WILLIAM J. SCHEICK

The Splintering Frame: The Later Fiction of H. G. Wells

**ELS
EDITIONS**

© 1984 by William J. Scheick
ELS Editions
Department of English
University of Victoria
Victoria, BC
Canada V8W 3W1
www.elseditions.com

Founding Editor: Samuel L. Macey

General Editor: Luke Carson

Printed by CreateSpace

English literary studies monograph series
ISSN 0829-7681 ; 31
ISBN-10 0-920604-15-3
ISBN-13 978-0-920604-15-1

For Catherine

CONTENTS

PREFACE

To remark that the novels of H. G. Wells merit serious critical discussion can still raise eyebrows; and even among the converted, the notion that Wells's best work includes some of his later discursive novels of ideas might seem perverse. The former reaction is slowly on its way to extinction, chiefly as a consequence of the good comments on Wells's work provided by Bernard Bergonzi, David Lodge, and William Bellamy,[1] among others. The latter reaction, however, remains steadfast at the moment in spite of recent pioneer efforts by Robert Bloom and Robert Philmus to raise the status of Wells's later writings.[2] My study focusses on Wells's fiction of the 1920's and 1930's, and my goal, put simply, is to deepen our appreciation of Wells as a literary artist.

Any discussion of Wells's literary artistry necessarily entails a consideration of his ideas. However, only a few of these ideas are explored here, primarily his concept of time and of the human will. Although I believe I have arrived at a reasonably accurate understanding of his views on time and will, the fact is that Wellsian concepts often remain problematical. For Wells was in effect less a thinker than a man thinking, which is to say that his thought is protean and, he liked to claim in his later years, self-consciously revisionary. In short, the scholar must be most cautious in any attempt at codifying or systematizing Wells's ideas.

Judged superficially, Wells's ideas might be dismissed as contradictory, or, perhaps, as confused; but a more precise scrutiny suggests a life-long devotion to dialectic, even at times to a sense of life as so fundamentally paradoxical that an artistic or philosophic rendering of reality requires the unresolved juxtaposition of opposites or of unlimited alternatives.[3] Even in his earliest writings Wells used the expression "opposite idea" to signify "essential complement" rather than "antithesis," a concept similar to Nietzsche's *Spannung*—an unsynthesizing contrast in which each term is meaningful only as it also points to the other.[4] In his later writings the same concept of mutually constitutive oppositions informs his vehement objections to Hegelian dialectic, which he thought overly stressed opposition as well as the possibility of synthesis. Wells was mistaken in many ways in his understanding of Hegelian dialectic, to which he was much

7

more indebted than he knew or cared to admit.[5] Moreover, Wells's manner, derived from his belief in essential complements, suited his employment of the ideas of others, ideas sometimes appropriated outrightly, sometimes presented surreptitiously or attributed mistakenly, sometimes deliberately modified or unwittingly misapprehended. All of this and more (a tendency toward vagueness, for example) contribute to the mazelike intricacies of Wells's views, including those on time and will.

Nevertheless, the reasons for general critical insensitivity to Wells's ideology and artistry run deeper than these complexities in his expression of ideas. In part the neglect of Wells's ideology and artistry derives from a belief, perhaps expressed best by Virginia Woolf, that a division occurred among novelists during the early twentieth century, a division between an Edwardian and a modern sensibility. For whatever reasons, this notion of a division took hold of the modern critical imagination, and in conjunction with the influence of Jamesian aesthetics and the emergence of New Criticism the values it implied, especially the preference for characterization over fictional structure,[6] became invincible orthodoxy.

Another cardinal factor in the neglect of Wells's ideas and writings was the aftershock of both World Wars. Whereas from 1895 to 1905, the year in which *A Modern Utopia* and *Kipps* appeared,[7] Wells's critical reception was on the rise, from 1915 to 1946 he experienced a decline in critical approval. The time between 1906 and 1914 comprised a period of transition for Wells, whose work during these years became increasingly explicit in its ideology. During this time, and after, the "politics" of his writings aroused a host of detractors: Roman Catholics, communists, fascists, and socialists, among others. In effect this vociferous reaction probably had no influence upon the declension of Wells's status today; indeed, I suspect that such notoriety only augmented it, then as well as now. Beyond such specific political rancor and beyond the emergence of a class of specialists who have discredited generalists of Wells's sort, lies a more fundamental attribute of his ideology that has certainly tarnished his image: his optimistic faith in a communal evolutionary progress underscored by a Romantic affirmation of the human self. Wells asserted this faith even through the 1920's and 1930's, when the aftermath of the War and of economic depression yielded a reactionary literary sentiment on the whole directly opposed to his belief.

To anyone who has struggled with Wells's thought, an unqualified critical stress on Wellsian optimism, on his belief in something akin to eighteenth-century post-millenialism, might seem less unfair than ironic: ironic because beneath the surface of so much of Wells's work, early and

8

late, there exists an abiding pessimism.[8] This pessimism, like George Gissing's and Thomas Hardy's, reflects a Darwinian influence, an influence vying with Wells's unconscious tendency to prefer a Lamarckian sense of evolution that is less pessimistic. It is most pronounced, perhaps, in the early work, especially whenever Wells resorts to a catastrophic event or to an extrinsic occurrence with the semblance of catastrophe in order to effect a miracle-like transformation of humanity. In the later works the event is more intrinsic and somewhat less catastrophic—a ghostly appearance from the quarry of human memory or the emergence of a subversive species within *Homo sapiens*—but the underlying sense remains the same, the implication that humanity is essentially unable to regenerate itself consciously by will. The despair and the open-ended structure which have made *Tono-Bungay* (1909) critically popular in some circles today are balanced by the optimistic promise of change and the satisfying ending of *The History of Mr. Polly* (1910). This apparent seesaw in Wells's attitude never ceased, though it became less extreme as he grew older. In short, Wells's asserted belief in the possibility of a utopian tomorrow contested with his personal sense of frustration, which sense for him also defined the *zeitgeist* of his day. Little wonder that late in his career he adapted certain concepts expressed by Oswald Spengler and Arthur Schopenhauer. As he remarked in *The New Machiavelli* (1911), "all history, all literature that matters, all science, deals with [the] conflict of the thing that is and the speculative 'if' that will destroy it" (W, 14: 211). Despair over the thing that is and faith in the speculative "if" abide in unresolved dialectic in Wells's work, and so the extensive critical debate concerning Wells's polarization towards one or the other side has been fruitless. However, in terms of popular reaction to him and his work, Wells's asserted optimism from mid-career to just before the end of his life struck many with greater force than the, by then, more muted pessimism. And this perception has helped to turn attention away from Wells's books and ideas.

Like that of Ralph Waldo Emerson, Wells's reputation as a serious artist has been damaged by modern critical antipathy to this perceived optimism in his writings. A hope in something ultimately benign and structured in the destiny of humanity was less tenable for most of the prominent thinkers and writers after World War I, and was further diminished after World War II. The comparison to Emerson is not capricious, for much that is Romantic and Transcendental informs Wells's scientific and fictional work at its deepest levels. His later works often refer to a mystical apprehension of reality, and in one noteworthy instance

9

Wells echoes a Keatsean sense of "truth and loveliness [as] primary things" (AD, 285). Doubtless such features, as much as any other factors, account for Wells's loss of status from 1914 to 1946; today this very mysticism might be valued, especially in light of the recent "disclosure" of the underlying correspondence between modern physics and traditional mysticism.[9] From time to time I shall remark Wells's Romanticism, but this component of his art, however worthy of concentrated focus, is confined within my broader aims.

These prefatory comments suggest finally that Wellsian ideology and artistry have been neglected partly because of what they are and partly because of what we have perceived them to be. In fact, I believe, a sound case can be found for the modernity of both his ideas and his artistic practice, especially late in his career when heightened self-awareness encouraged him to conduct remarkable experiments with the structure of the novel. To observe these experiments in his fiction of the 1920's and 1930's advances Wells's literary reputation; it also specifically narrows the gap between the Edwardian and the modern novelists as well as generally clarifies better the transition from Victorian to modern and contemporary fiction. (In this study I use the terms Victorian, Edwardian, modern, post-modern, and contemporary—in short, the vocabulary of established literary scholarship—as a form of shorthand, though in fact these terms disguise polymorphic complexities in the fiction of the periods they presumably define.)[10]

*　　*　　*

As my previous books have taught me, every work of this sort incurs debts. I acknowledge my indebtedness to the University Research Institute of the University of Texas at Austin for a grant providing me with the valuable time needed to complete this project.

I am also grateful to my colleagues in the Department of English, University of Texas at Austin: to Jerome Bump, John Farrell, Betty Sue Flowers, Alan Friedman, R. James Kaufmann, Charles Rossman, Ramón Saldívar, and William Todd for responding to various queries; and to Walter Reed and Wayne Rebhorn for somehow finding the time to comment on portions of this work while in manuscript.

Support came as well from other colleagues and friends: Richard Hauer Costa, Texas A&M University; David DeLaura, University of Pennsylvania; Robert F. Whitman, University of Pittsburgh; and the late Harris Wilson, University of Illinois at Urbana.

Since publication is a strong incentive, I wish to thank editors Jean-Claude Amalric, Jack I. Biles, Brad Grissom, H. E. Gerber, Robert M. Philmus, and Leonard Tennenhouse for publishing earlier versions of portions of this study. I am most indebted to the late H. E. Gerber, whose sponsorship of *English Literature in Transition* has nurtured serious scholarly interest in the Edwardians and whose strong support of my work on Wells for more than a decade accounts for this book as much as does any other factor.

I am especially grateful to Catherine Rainwater, who aided and abetted in the perpetration of this book.

ABBREVIATIONS FOR WORKS BY WELLS

Citations of works by H. G. Wells are inserted in parentheses directly into the text, immediately following a quotation or reference. Each citation can be identified by the abbreviations below, with its volume (when appropriate) and page number.

AA   *All Aboard for Ararat*. New York: Alliance Book Co., 1941.

AD   *Apropos of Dolores*. New York: Scribner's Sons, 1938.

AF   *The Anatomy of Frustration: A Modern Synthesis*. New York: Macmillan, 1936.

AP   *The Autocracy of Parham: His Remarkable Adventures in This Changing World*. Garden City, New York: Doubleday, Doran & Co., 1930.

Bro   *The Brothers*. London: Chatto & Windus, 1938.

Bry   *Brynhild; or The Show of Things*. New York: Scribner's Sons, 1937.

BB   *The Bulpington of Blup: Adventures, Poses, Stresses, Conflicts, and Disaster in a Contemporary Brain*. London: Hutchinson, 1932 .

BD   *Babes in the Darkling Wood*. New York: Alliance Book Co., 1940.

CA   *Christina Alberta's Father*. New York: Macmillan, 1925.

CP   *The Croquet Player: A Story*. London: Chatto & Windus, 1936.

CT   *The Conquest of Time*. London: Watts, 1942.

CV   *The Camford Visitation*. London: Methuen, 1937.

EA   *Experiment in Autobiography*. New York: Macmillan, 1934.

FM   *The Fate of Man*. New York: Longmans, Green, 1939.

HT   *The Holy Terror*. London: Michael Joseph, 1939.

KW   *The King Who Was a King: An Unconventional Novel*. Garden City, New York: Doubleday, Doran & Co., 1929.

M   *Meanwhile: The Picture of a Lady*. New York: Doran, 1927.

MB   *Mr. Blettsworthy on Rampole Island*. Garden City, New York: Doubleday, Doran & Co., 1928.

NA   *The New America: The New World.* London: Cresset, 1935.

OC   *The Open Conspiracy: Blueprints for a World Revolution.* Garden City, New York: Doubleday, Doran & Co., 1928.

OH   *The Outline of History.* New York: Macmillan, 1921.

SB   *Star Begotten: A Biological Fantasia.* London: Chatto & Windus, 1937.

W   *The Works of H. G. Wells.* Atlantic Edition. New York: Scribner's Sons, 1924-1927. 28 volumes.

    Vol. 9: "The Contemporary Novel."

    Vol. 11: *The Undying Fire.*

    Vol. 12: *Tono-Bungay.*

    Vol. 13: *Boon.*

    Vol. 14: *The New Machiavelli.*

    Vol. 17: *The History of Mr. Polly.*

    Vol. 18: *Men Like Gods* and *The Dream.*

WB   *World Brain.* Garden City, New York: Doubleday, Doran & Co., 1938.

WC   *The World of William Clissold: A Novel at a New Angle.* New York: Doran, 1926.

WH   *The Work, Wealth, and Happiness of Mankind.* London: Heinemann, 1932.

YC   *You Can't Be Too Careful: A Sample of Life.* New York: Putnam's Sons, 1942.

CHAPTER I

The Splintering Frame

The Shape of a Literary Career

Wells's career as a novelist, according to the majority of sympathetic literary critics, reached its apogee with the publication of *Tono-Bungay* in 1909 and *The History of Mr. Polly* in the following year. According to these critics, after 1910, the year designated by Virginia Woolf as the time of transition from Edwardian to more modern literary standards, Wells's artistic achievement declined rapidly. Bernard Bergonzi, who has written informatively on Wells's early fiction, expresses this consensus: "Wells, at the beginning of his career, was a genuine artist, who wrote several books of considerable literary importance, before dissipating in directions which now seem more or less irrelevant."[1]

This prevalent attitude should be reconsidered. Oddly, it does not correspond to Wells's own assessment of his career. In the prefatory matter to the edition of his collected works (1924-27) he declares highest regard for several of his later writings, in his autobiography (1934) he expressly devalues his early fiction in comparison to his most recent works, and in the novels he wrote during his last decade—e.g., *The Anatomy of Frustration* (1936) and *Star Begotten* (1937)—he alludes, often humorously, to the best known of his early books in order to intimate an ideological and artistic revisionism in the text in hand as well as to dispel the expectations engendered in readers by his early works. Wells might have been myopic regarding his own works. However, Wells's opinion that his later fiction manifests an artistic self-consciousness and execution far superior to the sometimes allegorical, sometimes satirical manner of his early romances can be supported by a contextual review of his work.

Such a review reveals, for instance, that *Tono-Bungay* anticipates his later fiction in both ideas and manner. Curiously, critics overlook this relationship—curiously because defenders of *Tono-Bungay* tend to labor hard when advancing a case for authorial artistic self-consciousness in the novel. Their essentially defensive posture derives from a silent or acknowledged conviction that virtually everything Wells wrote afterwards is artistically deficient. Defenders of *Tono-Bungay* struggle against debunking commentary, such as that of Mark Schorer's on the book,[2] because their arguments exist *in vacuo* and upon occasion are vitiated by latent self-doubt.

Consider a recent study of the novel, a thoughtful and useful essay by Lucille Herbert, contending that *Tono-Bungay* is an original and unified novel. Although Herbert's discussion improves upon previous efforts to define the artistic merits of the book, it includes an undercurrent of critical doubt. This uncertainty becomes detectable when Herbert prudently confesses that she would like to believe Ponderevo to be an unreliable narrator in the novel, to be an ironic victim of the very social malaise he diagnoses, but finds insufficient evidence to sustain her belief.[3] Herbert's honesty is admirable, but such uncertainties, against her critical desire and need, to some degree undermine her claim for the level of Wells's artistic success in the novel. Part of the problem lies in her insistence upon unity as a critical standard; she fails to appreciate fully the contrapuntal rhythm and the ongoing dialectical revisionism characteristic of this novel. Considering *Tono-Bungay* in the context of the fiction Wells wrote later would highlight these traits.

Herbert's recognition of authorial artistic consciousness in *Tono-Bungay* is indeed supportable. Over ten years ago Kenneth Newell and I demonstrated one feature of Wells's conscious artistic control: his use of motif as a structuring device.[4] Even then, though probably instinctively, I sensed the value of conducting my investigation of *Tono-Bungay* in a context provided by *In the Days of the Comet* (1906) and *The Undying Fire* (1919), thereby to suggest continuity in Wells's practice. Wells, it is safe to say, was an inveterate user of motifs as an unobtrusive unifying device throughout his entire literary career.[5] However, the observation of this fact, it seems to me now, proves too limited in an assessment of his literary talent. Compared with English and American novels generally regarded as major examples of *belles-lettres*, Wells's fiction exhibits motifs which are usually univalent rather than multivalent. His motifs often lack richness and range, so that while the recognition of Wells's management of motifs supports the argument for conscious artistry in his fiction, it fails to advance that claim very far on behalf of the overall achievement of his art.

Wells's literary art might be better described by means of a method emphasizing the relation of specific ideas to his experimentation with fictional conventions, as he perceived them, and to his search for a revolutionary form for the novel. Herbert implies such an approach when suggesting that the narrator of *Tono-Bungay* "requires a new language

15

and a new form for which he can find no models. Thus the essential and unifying form of *Tono-Bungay* becomes that of a search for expression which inheres in the process of composition itself."[6] This and so much more is true not only of *Tono-Bungay* but generally of Wells's fiction after that novel. Throughout his career Wells was irritated by the limits he perceived in the fictional conventions he inherited. His understanding of the nature of these conventions, or repertoire of the novel, did not differ from that of Virginia Woolf, who spoke of them as mechanisms whereby a writer "get[s] into touch with his reader by putting before him something which he recognizes, which therefore stimulates his imagination, and makes him willing to cooperate in the far more difficult business of intimacy."[7] Like Thomas Hardy in *Jude the Obscure* (1895) and Joseph Conrad in *Lord Jim* (1900), however, Wells also pondered the ideological implications of prevalent fictional conventions, particularly the degree to which they reflect and perpetuate delimiting social illusions. This perception of fictional conventions informed his search for strategies in narrative technique, principally in the management of structure, authorial omniscience, character portrayal, and plot closure. More appropriate to Wells's social and artistic beliefs, these deliberate strategies opposed readers' conditioned expectations and thereby exposed each reader's tendency to "naturalize" every narrative convention, "not only to understand it, but to 'forget' its conventional character, to absorb it into the reading-out process, to incorporate it into one's interpretive net, giving to it no more thought than to the manifestational medium."[8]

Early in his career as a writer this concern with fictional conventions was not acute. Then he wrote relatively straightforward stories, often with allegorical overtones, emphasizing plot and evincing principally Swiftian and Dickensian influences. Certainly Wells demonstrated originality in these works as well as revealed a knack for imitating successful literary techniques. This latter talent found expression primarily in satiric or parodic treatments of specific texts as well as in deliberate distortions or inversions of various conventions of the Victorian novel. *Tono-Bungay*, for example, so recasts the recurrent fictional preoccupation with the search for a father that the protagonist's eventual pessimistic awareness of an essential rootlessness in life reflects the more pervasive disorder of post-Victorian culture.[9] In the same year Wells violated the Victorian fictional convention of the saintly woman in *Ann Veronica* (1909).[10] Actually Wells conducted similar experiments much earlier. *When the Sleeper Wakes* (1899) parodies the inheritance convention of Victorian fiction,[11] and *The Food of the Gods* (1904) deftly manages reader

16

response so that the sympathy given to ordinary humanity in the first half of the book is transferred to the giants, who threaten that ordinary world, in the second half.[12] *In the Days of the Comet*, published two years later, reveals a similarly distinctive division: whereas the first part of the work recalls the Victorian suspense novel, the second half fails to fulfill expectations engendered by the preceding section, thereby forcing the reader "into an analytic mode in the very act of processing his own 'literary' reactions, his fictional disappointments."[13] These observations, each made by a critic independently of the findings of the others, collectively testify to an artistic self-awareness in Wells considerably beyond that generally attributed to him. This evidence, it might be further noted, is underscored by the deft management of framing in *The Time Machine* (1895),[14] the inversion of the conventions of the imperialist romance in *The Island of Dr. Moreau* (1896) and *The War of the Worlds* (1897), the reversal in *Bealby* (1915) of Smollett's pattern in *The Expedition of Humphrey Clinker* (1771), and the use of art to question art, specifically to explore the consequences of the aesthetic impulse, in *The History of Mr. Polly*.[15]

Never satisfied with mere imitation, Wells preferred parody, distortion and satire. Initially his antagonism toward established literary conventions might have originated from a youthful impulse to treat the "sacred" givens of Victorian fiction sacrilegiously, from a desire to startle readers out of their complacent expectations and to impress upon them a sense of his own cleverness, or from a typical Wellsian craving for something different. But as his career took shape and matured, he became increasingly convinced of the inappropriateness of the prevalent mode of the novel to the ideas he wished to express — ideas he desired to present both journalistically and aesthetically through the vehicle of fiction. This awareness resulted in a search for suitable fictional forms. This search channeled and intensified Wells's artistic sensibility; and although such a sensibility was no guarantee of aesthetic achievement, in Wells's case they went hand in hand.

When the Sleeper Wakes, through *Tono-Bungay*, to *Bealby* delineates the period during which Wells's consciousness as a literary artist awakened, especially concerning fictional conventions and reader expectations. Wells would assign 1920 as the date marking the maturation of this awareness. The works he published before *When the Sleeper Wakes*, however beloved by most of Wells's critics, seem on the whole more casual in contrast to many of the subsequent writings. Even as late as 1905, he could rely on an utterly conventional Victorian plot-structure for *Kipps*.[16]

Although Wells's fictional art apparently did not develop in any neatly linear manner, development indeed occurred and reached maturity in the Twenties and Thirties. This development revealed a noteworthy moment in 1915, the year *Bealby* was followed by *Boon* with its merciless attack on Henry James's novels. The controversy between Wells and James is well known,[17] and a rehearsal of its details is not required here. For our purposes we need only recall Wells's disparagement of James's alleged total preoccupation with unity and form in fiction as ends in themselves. "If the novel is to follow life it must be various and discursive," Wells proclaimed in *Boon*, "life is diversity and entertainment, not completeness and satisfaction" (W, 13:454).

By 1915, the discursive novel had become Wells's *métier*. In fact he had explicitly defended it as early as 1911, in an essay entitled "The Contemporary Novel." The discursive mode, even when used in reply to Jamesian aesthetics, does not necessarily imply a lack of form. Wells's employment of motifs, his admission to having relied upon "types and symbols" (EA, 414), besides other evidence, attest to the fact that his discursive fiction aimed for a certain formal coherence. The primary question plaguing Wells by 1915 was: Just *what* form suited his fictional purposes? From 1915 to 1922, he mastered a modification of Platonic dialogue—a non-fictional form with tangencies to the novel—an undertaking Wells described in his later years as "only one of the directions in which I have wandered away from the uncongenial limitations of the novel proper" (EA, 420). The results of this adaptation are uneven, and it is after the appearance of *The Secret Places of the Heart* (1922) that Wells's search for appropriate fictional forms yields a more consistent aesthetic richness in his fiction.

In other words, Wells's maturation as a writer coincides with the rise of modernism in the early Twenties. Wells came to see his career in this way. In *World Brain* (1938) he designates 1920 as a turning point in the human mind as well as the date of his own intellectual ripening (WB, 6, 98), a view mirrored in *The Anatomy of Frustration* when William Burroughs Steele is reported to have commenced his major work in 1922. In *World Brain* Wells observes: "The thoughts I am setting out here have troubled my mind for years, and my ideas have been slowly gathering definition throughout these experiments and experiences" (WB, 5). This clarification of focus applied as well to his art. "It required some years and a number of ... experiments and essays in statement," he explained in 1934, "before I got really clear in my own mind that I was feeling my way towards something outside any established formula for the novel altogether" (EA, 418). During the Thirties Wells's fiction and thought were inextricably intertwined. The brilliance of his work during this decade, when his earlier antagonism toward fictional conventions transformed itself most completely into artistic innovation, is founded on his authorial self-awareness and his clarification of ideas in his novels during the Twenties, novels which were experiments with fictional techniques reflecting his sense of the effect of World War I, modern thought and modern technology on Western civilization.

The Fourth Dimension

In the minds of many of Wells's contemporaries, the Twenties expressed a reaction to the rigid framework of values determining the social order of the pre-War years. The pre-War façade, they agreed, conveyed an illusion of stability that stifled independent thought and concealed a latent hypocrisy. At the heart of their response was the rejection of the notion that the War provided an opportunity to regenerate civilization, that "old Bitch gone in the teeth," as Ezra Pound saw it. To many, in short, authority and tradition had collapsed as the structured world-view of the pre-War years seemed to collapse into chaotic freedom. This freedom was not perceived by all to be intrinsically redeeming. As Joseph Wood Krutch's very popular *The Modern Temper* (1929) indicates, the exposure of the limits of humanism, the disillusionment with science, the death of value and of tragedy, the failure of art—in sum, the exposure of "the phantom of certitude" leaves humanity bereft of any trust in reason, will, or love, which in fact disguise respectively mere rationalization, conditioned reflex, and biological urge. "Ours is a lost cause and there is no place for us in the natural universe, but we are not, for all that, sorry to be human," Krutch concluded; for

> if Humanism and Nature are fundamentally antithetical, if the human virtues have a definite limit set to their development, and if they may be cultivated only by a process which renders us progressively unfit to fulfill our biological duties, then we at least permit ourselves a certain defiant satisfaction when we realize that we have made our choice and that we are resolved to abide by the consequences. Some small part of the tragic fallacy may be said indeed to be still valid for us, for if we cannot feel ourselves great as Shakespeare did, if we no longer believe in either our infinite capacities or own importance to the universe, we know at least that we discovered the trick which has been played upon us and that whatever else we may be we are no longer dupes.[18]

In Krutch's opinion, as in Wells's, science poses a particular threat to humanity whenever it is reverenced for assurances which claim to fill the void left by the destruction of traditional sources of value, a notion also prominent in C. E. Ayres's *Science, The False Messiah* (1927). Even the genial Albert Einstein was not exempt from attack resulting from this distrust of science. In "Einstein" (1929), a poem by Archibald MacLeish, the famous physicist emerges as a figure of pathetic and self-defeating defiance. Popularization of Einstein's General Theory of Relativity commenced in 1919. This theory, explained too simply, held that all motion is relative to two systems or frames of reference, with the consequence that space and time are not separate but comprise a four-dimensional continuum. Wells was familiar with this theory and on one occasion not only demonstrated a keen awareness of it but also claimed that he had anticipated it in a somewhat crude form.[19] He had read Einstein's *Relativity* (1918; trans. 1920) as well as Ludwig Silberstein's *The Theory of Relativity* (1914) (WH, 76), and he wrote "A Summary of Modern Ideas about Space and Time," appended to his *The Conquest of Time* (1942), a lucid explanation of his own understanding of the fourth dimension. Elsewhere Wells spoke of Einstein, with whom he privately exchanged views during a meeting sometime after the War (EA, 655), as the man "who upset all our ideas of space and time" (WH, 772), an opinion recalling the distrust of science during the Twenties.

He was similarly aware of other concepts of modern physics. He knew of Nobel Prize winner Max Planck's hypothesis, refuting the cause-and-effect thesis of classical physics and defining the random principle of quantum theory, that oscillating atoms absorb and emit energy only in discrete bundles instead of continuously. Reflecting on Planck's *Where is Science Going?* (1932), for which Einstein wrote a prologue, Wells skeptically pondered the author's belief that "we must fall back on our Faith that ultimately finer measurements and a closer analysis will eliminate [the] quality of indeterminateness" revealed by modern physics (EA, 179). Wells doubted that such an ordered framework in the old-fashioned sense implied by Planck informs the physical world or that whatever transcendent principle of order might inform creation is accessible to the mind of any individual: "The past and the future *exist permanently* in this universe, and our consciousness is a series of delusively unified conditioned reflexes" (CT, 83-84). As early as 1891 he had argued, in "The Rediscovery of the Unique," that in nature, which never repeats itself, only approximate similarities occur. Later too he applauded

Sir James Jeans, who in *The Mysterious Universe* (1930) observed, according to Wells, " 'loose jointedness' of any type whatever pervad[ing] the whole universe, destroys the case for absolute strict causation, the latter being the characteristic of perfectly fitted machinery" (EA, 181). Two years earlier Wells combined the concepts of Jeans and of Einstein to conclude: "The realization by the world of mathematical physics that the universe can be represented as a four-dimensional universe of unique events had abolished the conception of a quantitative equivalence of cause and effect and made every atom unique" (WH, 69)—a disclosure similar to that of evolution in its implication of "no strict limits set" for the human species. The concepts of relativity and indeterminacy figure significantly in Wells's experiments with fictional structure during the "Twenties and Thirties.[20]

Wells's interest in the fourth dimension actually pre-dates the popularization of Einstein's General Theory of Relativity after 1919. He and his fellow students at South Kensington had discussed four-dimensional geometry (CT, 71). He was about eighteen when, according to his recollection, he first encountered the notion of "time being space": "There were three dimensions, up and down, fore and aft and right and left, and I never heard of a fourth dimension until 1884 or thereabout" (EA, 70). In 1884 the English theologian Edwin A. Abbott published a tale entitled *Flatland: A Romance of Many Dimensions*. This satirical work recounts the vision of three-dimensional space experienced by an inhabitant of two-dimensional Flatland; it raises the possibility of an infinitesimal "Fourth Dimension," where one might look upon the third dimension "and see the inside of every three-dimensional house, the secrets of the solid earth, the treasures of the mines in Spaceland, and the intestines of every solid living creature."[21] Whether or not Wells had read *Flatland*, there were ample opportunities for him to encounter similar theories about the fourth dimension in the earliest stages of his career. He reviewed, for the *Sunday Review*,[22] George MacDonald's *Lilith* (1896), which suggests that any number of three-dimensional worlds might exist in a fourth-dimensional one. Before and shortly after the turn of the century Charles Howard Hinton published *A New Era of Thought* (1888), a theoretical treatise on the fourth dimension; *Scientific Romances* (1884-85), in which "What Is the Fourth Dimension?" was reprinted from the *Dublin University Magazine* (1880); and *Scientific Romances, Second Series* (1909), which poses the possibility that just as dimensionality informs nature, it may characterize human thought. P. D. Ouspensky whom Wells mentions in passing in *The Bulpington of Blup*

21

(1932) (BB, 369), published *The Fourth Dimension* in 1909 and a pertinent volume of *Tertium Organum* in 1911. And Henri Bergson had, in *L'evolution créative* (1907) and elsewhere, advanced arguments about duration and reality, a discussion anticipated by the philosophy of William James as well as by the practice of nineteenth-century novelists, and apparently highly influential on several novelists of the early twentieth century.[23] Articles on the fourth dimension appeared during these early years in such periodicals as *Current Literature, McClure's Magazine, The Popular Science Monthly,* and *Scientific American.* Moreover, and finally, it is relevant to recall that the theoretical basis for Cubism, the school of painting and sculpture developed in Paris during the early twentieth century, played with notions of the fourth dimension derived from non-Euclidean geometry as well as, according to Gertrude Stein (who did not identify the mathematical source), a modified view of reality: "the framing of life, the need that a picture exist in its frame, remain in its frame was over. A picture remaining in its frame was a thing that always had existed and now pictures commenced to want to leave their frames and this also created the necessity for cubism."[24]

These early speculations about the artistic expressions of the fourth dimension differ from Einstein's theory in several aspects, most particularly in presenting the three-dimensional world as merely a portion or part of a four-dimensional reality where time exists *spatially.* Whereas in these early accounts time is considered a fixed feature of four-dimensional space, in Einstein's theory time alone comprises the fourth dimension and makes space fluid. Einstein's theory and its predecessors converge at least at one point: like Guillaume Apollinaire, who considered the Cubist revelation of the fourth dimension as a way to overcome "that miserable tricky perspective," and like Maurice Raynal, who concluded that Cubist artists conveyed this dimension by "painting objects as they *thought* them,"[25] Einstein stressed individual perception, or relativity. Wells, who continually decried "the subjective and illusory point of view" of the individual (CT, 84), similarly explained: "Our yesterdays and tomorrows, our hopes and fears, life and death, and all the sequences of our individual and specific life are no more than a moving picture set in the frame of Relativity" (CT, 42).

In 1894, in an essay printed in the *National Observer,* Wells discussed time as the fourth dimension of space, observing that "our consciousnesses, which are immaterial and have no dimensions, are passing along the time-dimension with a uniform velocity from the cradle to the grave."[26] In *The Time Machine* time serves metaphorically as a dimension open to the human imagination and prophecy.[27] Likewise in "The Remarkable Case of Davidson's Eyes," "The Plattner Story," and *The Wonderful Visit* (1895) the fourth dimension serves as a vehicle for social and political allegory. After these early works Wells's interest in time shifts away from novelty to the bedrock of history, a shift climaxed in *The Outline of History* (1920). The years 1919 and 1920, when Einstein's theory was popularized, signal a return of Wells's interest in time as the fourth dimension. Barely hinted at in *The Undying Fire*, this change emerges prominently in *Men Like Gods* (1923) and *The Dream* (1924). In these two novels and their successors Wells often specifically refers to the relativity of time to expose ideological and aesthetic implications. In these works, as in Lawrence Durrell's *Alexandria Quartet* (1957-60), time is no mere metaphor but a pervasive reality informing countless alternatives of human perspective and possibility. Late in life Wells devalued *The Time Machine* (CT, 71) specifically from this revised perspective, indicating that "not in any sort of metaphor but in actuality and reality, past and future are dissolving into an ever-expanding Now" (CT, 12). In time any event comprises simply one occurrence within an infinite number of parallel and arbitrary events close to it, as if (Wells explained) "an infinitude of three-dimensional systems [existed] side by side in a four-dimensional universe," "countless three-dimensional universes like the leaves of a book" (CT, 79, 80). In the last two decades of his life Wells correlates time, in the abstract, with an hypothetical collective human perspective: finite yet open to infinite alternatives, and therefore disclosing a promise of potential ongoing human attainment. In Wells's own words, "the picture of the physical nature of things Einstein develops is of a universe that completely returns into itself, and is therefore *finite*"; yet, paradoxically, "the universe, the frame of life in space and time, expands with our knowledge, [and] it expands without apparent limit" (CT, 83, 63).

This extrapolation from Einstein's theory, besides other disclosures of modern physics typified by Planck's discoveries and Arthur S. Eddington's *The Expanding Universe* (1931) (CT, 83), informs Wells's treatment of fictional conventions in the novels he wrote during the Twenties and the Thirties. If he did not endorse the pessimism many of the spokesmen of these two decades derived from scientific findings, he did share with important artists of the time a sense that the artistic conventions of the preceding generations were as defunct as was the ideological framework supporting them. Moreover, he identified a hierarchical range in the arts based on their dimensionality; he asserted that painting and

23

photography were two-dimensional, sculpture and architecture three dimensional, music and literature four dimensional (CT, 79). In its aesthetic possibilities, Wells believed, fiction held forth special promise for an author's effort to awaken humanity to its potential destiny. This attitude toward fiction informs the maturation of Wells's artistry during his later years. During the Twenties and Thirties Wells sought to subject the conventions of fiction—as it were, the "space" of fiction—to the relativity of the reader, to make fictional "space" manifest a fourth dimension of timeliness, or relevance, to the reader.

In the last years of his life he referred to this as yet unspecified technique as "the splintering frame." This image recalls Gertrude Stein's description of Cubism and echoes Wells's statements on the effect of World War I on Western civilization and of modern science upon mankind's world view. Before the War, as Wells explained in 1934, there seemed to be "a rigid frame of values never more to be questioned or permanently changed," and accordingly the "standards [of the English novel] were established within that apparently permanent frame." But since the War, he continued, criticism of the novel "began to be irritated and perplexed when, through a new instability, the splintering frame began to get into the picture." Wells was, in his own words, "for a time ... the outstanding instance among writers of fiction in English of the frame getting into the picture" (EA, 416). For Wells, fiction with a "splintering frame" reflected post-War reality; and Bernard Bergonzi rightly observes in passing that "Wells's striking image ... though meant to apply to his own fictional activities, can also refer to the great Modernist innovations in twentieth-century fiction."[28] This frame was beyond repair: "We are, as a species, caught in an irreversible process. No real going back to the old, comparatively stable condition of things is possible"; this less stable or splintering condition is now "a part of the frame in which our lives are set" (EA, 197).

The aesthetic design of Wells's late fiction conveys this new reality of "the frame of Relativity" (CT, 42), which evokes hope rather than despair concerning human potentiality. This concern in his work is reinforced by techniques—related to yet distinct from other modernist experiments with "open form";[29] these techniques were to make this reality thematically pertinent to each reader's relativity, or perspective. In this way Wells hoped to achieve "a kinetic art ... reorient[ed] ... from within" (AF, 202). Specifically, Wells's technique of "the splintering frame" employs certain fictional conventions in a way designed (a) to frustrate expectations aroused by these conventions, (b) to draw attention to the

24

artificiality of and ideology behind these conventions, and (c) to point away from the "exhausted" text as a self-contained, finished artifact and towards the self-aware reader, who ideally participates within the expanded boundary of the text and discovers within himself a capacity (dimensionality) for a heightened awareness of and control over human fate. This technique of the splintering frame comprises the aesthetic fourth dimension of Wells's novels.

To achieve this aesthetic fourth dimension in his late fiction—this subjection of fictional "space" or convention to reader timeliness, relevance or relativity—Wells created an emergent interior structure which dialectically engages (in a mutually constitutive opposition) a more apparent exterior structure; in the process the exterior structure of his novels is expanded and is reformed/re-formed. The emergent inner structure is, for Wells, artistically equivalent to time, dream, or a dimensionality encompassing countless alternatives of human possibility. The emergence of the interior structure splinters the frame of the exterior structure in a late Wells novel, even as (in Wells's view) the insight given by World War I fractured the extrinsic framework of social values in Western civilization. This rupture expands and revises the exterior structure (literary convention) as well as the reader's expectations and sense of reality. Ideally both reformed structure and modified reader sensibility become four dimensional or, in other words, open to ever-expanding indeterminate possibilities. The reader's experience of this revision of fictional convention and reader expectation parallels Wells's personal revision of ideas in his novels. Intrinsically utilitarian, this double revision represents the product of Wells's mature management of fictional structure, a management conforming to the idea, which he expressed to Henry James on 8 July 1915, that "literature like architecture is a means, it has a use."[30]

Typological Characterization

In the modern period, then, Wells was as interested in time in fiction as were James Joyce and Virginia Woolf. For Joyce and Woolf, however, time is a function of the psychological processes of their characters. Maintaining a view similar to Henri Bergson's idea of *dureé* and advancing the practice of nineteenth-century novelists like Henry James, Joyce and Woolf conveyed time in their works through a stream of impressions, thoughts, images as filtered through a perceiving self. Wells could appreciate the use of such perceiving intelligences in fiction; he had in fact written a favorable and influential review of Joyce's *A Portrait of the Artist as a Young*

Man (1916). But Wells was sure that the Modernist's application of time theory to individual subjective perception, while accurate in a psychological sense, was inadequate. He posited a larger, more objective "collective time" of which (he believed) individuals generally remain ignorant because, simply, a part cannot know the whole of which it is a part. Nevertheless, sometimes transient near-mystical intimations of this "collective time" are experienced by certain individuals, who become in Wells's fiction unlikely prophets of human destiny.

Wells spoke of this broader perspective as a hypothetical absolute viewpoint. Among his earliest writings is an essay, printed in the *New Review* (1895), arguing, "From the absolute point of view the universe is a perfectly rigid unalterable apparatus, entirely complete and finished."[31] Later in life when he was influenced by Albert Einstein and Arthur Eddington, Wells came to believe the finite universe was expanding infinitely, but he never abandoned the notion that from a *hypothetical* absolute point of view a "rigid" principle of order informs this universe and that the individual in this universe achieves genuine identity in terms of a definition greater than that provided by the self: "consciousness of a self . . . *is a serviceable synthetic illusion of continuity that holds the individual behavior together*," and "there is another life far greater than the individual life . . . the life of the species as a whole" embodying a "collective will" (CT, 17, 35, 40). In *Star Begotten* he explained, "A new sort of mind *is* coming into the world, with a new, simpler, clearer and more powerful way of thinking," but "so far these new minds haven't got together for any sort of associated living" (SB, 139; cf. 172). Rather than total subordination of individuality or dogmatic individualism, Wells advocates "associated" individuals, an illustration of his understanding of "essential complements"; for "if a species survives, then it survives only by and through its individuals" (CT, 40). The individual was important to Wells, but only in the context of a collective human destiny.

What mattered to Wells in a novel was how much an exemplary or typical character's mind aligned with the collective mind of *Homo sapiens*, whose ever-expanding collective insight and destiny are (for Wells) relative (at any given moment in its history) to an infinitely expanding universe. The human mind and the physical universe comprise, for Wells, the two systems or frames of reference (spirit and matter, fate and freedom) exemplifying the relativity of motion and the four-dimensional continuum explained by Einstein: "all the sequences of our individual and specific life are no more than a moving picture set in the frame of Relativity"; "the universe, the frame of life in space and time, expands with our knowledge, but it expands without apparent limit" (CT, 42, 63). In this light Wells fashioned characters who are *individuals*, perceiving intelligences enjoying a delusive sense of personal freedom potentially fatal to the species; at the same time they are types conforming to a fate infused with a potentiality for advancing the species toward some greater collective perfection.

For Wells, characters ought to be like the average person: at once unique and typical. He had argued as early as 1891, in "The Rediscovery of the Unique," that in nature only approximate similarities occur; he repeated this idea as late as 1932, when he spoke of the implications of "a four-dimensional universe of unique events" (WH, 69). These remarks pertain to the physical world, where the "freedom" of the random atom comprises our "fate." They pertain to the biology determining the individuality of a person.

However, there is another side to this uniqueness. In 1895, Wells also explained: "the individuals perish, living on only in their descendents, creatures of their body, separated pieces of their undying protoplasm: the type alone persists."[32] Some principle of order informs nature, which expresses itself in uniqueness. As late as 1942, Wells was still considering the paradoxical interaction of the unique and the typical. "When that space time continuum [defined by Einstein] is considered as a whole," he explained, classifications of individuals or species surrender distinctions and "merge into one another," so that finally there is "a Type specimen and a series of variations" of that Type (CT, 42). This stress on the type, then, surfaced in Wells's early and late works. Even his autobiography demonstrates the concept in the following illustrative reflections: "In fact Adolf Hitler is nothing more than one of my thirteen year old reveries come real. A whole generation of Germans has failed to grow up" (EA, 75). Moving beyond his "Hitler phase," the "Hitlerite stage of [his own] development" (EA, 76, 80), he concludes, "my individual story merges into the story of the handicapped intelligence of the species, blundering heavily towards the realization and handling of vast changes and still vaster dangers and opportunities"; "my life is a sample life and not an exceptional one; its distinctive merit has been its expressiveness" (EA, 104).

Wells's preference for typical characters is disclosed in his very early praise of Thomas Hardy's *Jude the Obscure* for its depiction of a protagonist who is "at once an individual and a type."[33] In the same year, again in the *Saturday Review*, he spoke of Ivan Turgénev's *Fathers and Sons* (1861) as a "novel of types": "The peculiar characteristics of Tur-

27

génev's genius is the extraordinary way in which he can make his characters typical, while at the same time retaining their individuality"; "they
are living, breathing individuals, but individuals living under the full stress
of this great racial force or that."[34] Near the end of his career too Wells
described several of his own lesser fictional portraits as "caricature-
individualities" (EA, 420); but the phrase perfectly suits the mode of
characterization he practiced generally, even in his last novels, which are
much concerned with the interior life of protagonists.

The typical side of a late Wellsian character represents the species or
collective human mind, whereas the individual side represents egocentricity of self. Moreover, in Wells's correlation, individuality manifests a
mode of freedom obscuring a subservience to biology and threatening the
fate of the human species; in contrast, typicality signifies a conformity to
a collective fate ever expanding to the extent that it generates freedom
and possibility for the species as a whole. Caricature and individuality, it
follows, are not two distinct literary manners for Wells. They comprise
"essential complements," like freedom and fate, matter and spirit. All such
dialectical oppositions, as *The Anatomy of Frustration* indicates, constitute a dynamic unity. Humanity is spirit and matter, predestined and free.
Engaged in some dimensional interaction beyond human ken, each of
these mutually constitutive oppositions apparently transpose identities, so
that, metaphorically, matter becomes fluid through the warp of time (the
spirit of human relativity), so that the freedom of one generation becomes
the fate of the next—indeed, freedom in the sense of infinite expansion is
itself fated. In Wells's late fiction this paradox is manifested in the human
experience of fated limits, limits somehow mentally expandable yet also
eventually providing a new framework of fate, which in turn will again
need to be expanded, and so on in an infinite dialectical exchange between freedom and predestination in the human mind. Like Ralph Waldo
Emerson, in "Fate,"[35] Wells depicted humanity as always "framed" or
fated—humanity's real, not its myopically perceived, individual and material side; yet humanity always extends the range of freedom outward—
humanity's fated typical or spiritual side—*within* this realm of necessity.
This conception informs Wells's experimentation not only with structure,
the interior feature of which splinters and reforms/re-forms its framing
exterior feature, but also with a typological mode of characterization.

Wells's sense of proper characterization as a combination of typicality
and individuality echoes Engels and Marx, who both adopted Hegel's
view of the matter.[36] But the source is much older than Hegel and probably lies in Christian typological tradition, which begins with the com-

mentaries of the Church Fathers and climaxes in the Puritan culture of the seventeenth century. In this scheme a type refers to a particular kind of symbol, an historical or actual person, place, object or event in the Old Testament foreshadowing its antitype, its equally real and historical fulfillment or explanation in the New Testament. In most instances Christ is the antitype revealing the secret symbolic meaning of the shadows, images or signs presented in the Old Testament. Typology comprises a closed world of symbols with (presumably) no room for interpretation, although the more liberal school of typological thought allowed that the Old Testament types extend in allegorical implication beyond Christ to include every Christian until the Second Coming.[37]

Wells probably knew little, if anything, about the intricacies of typological tradition. Regardless of his consciousness of the history of this issue, however, he inherited an appreciation of literary allegory, which derived from this tradition. Moreover, even in its more restricted sense, typology persisted in the literature of the eighteenth and nineteenth centuries.[38] In early nineteenth-century America it informed Emerson's and Thoreau's attribution of a sacramentality to natural facts; in England it survived in the work of Thomas Carlyle and John Ruskin, who fused traditional biblical typology and the implications of modern science in order to translate fact into figure and thereby to disclose a transcendental dimension in facts. Among the Victorians, furthermore, Gerard Manley Hopkins employed the typological system in his poetry and, before him members of the early Pre-Raphaelite Brotherhood did likewise in their paintings, evoking through historical and contemporary details a sacred meaning to replace an exhausted cultural tradition.[39] Nor should we overlook George Eliot's *Adam Bede* (1859) or Hardy's *Tess of the D'Ubervilles* (1891) and *Jude the Obscure*, to cite only three examples of fiction in which typological characterization conveys a sense of history's repetition of itself.

Wells was especially fond of using biblical and historical figures who represent, in his opinion, recurrent fundamental types throughout time. Noteworthy modification distinguishes Wells's typology. Noah, Job, Christ, Sargon, among several others, reappear again and again; but unlike the static Jungean archetypes in Thomas Mann's tetralogy *Joseph und seine Bruder* (1933-43), in Wells's fiction these figures become successively more "evolved": "not an exact repetition," but "a parallel at another level" (AF, 46). This means that in lieu of an antitype there is in human history a succession of antitypes, each of which in turn is reduced to the status of a type prefiguring a fuller realization of its identity in the future. In this adaptation of the allegorical typological system, implying a firm teleological order, each successive antitype is paradoxically both typical and unique. They share an underlying typical identity; they also, in their respective phenomenological manifestations in particular periods of time, splinter the frame of that identity by displaying a slight variation which makes each "incarnation" unique. Their similarities unite them in a community transcending any particular individual manifestation of the type; yet these same similarities are finally only approximate, for each successive reappearance of any one type involves a Lamarckian progressive advancement in human cultural evolution.

Two Novels

At this point a brief consideration of two novels, written by Wells twenty-two years apart, should be clarifying.

All Aboard for Ararat (1941) is Wells's third last fictional work, a dialogue novel without a strong plot. An escapee from a mental asylum who calls himself God instructs Noah Lammock to build an ark in preparation for a world-wide devastating deluge (World War II). Noah demurs, but after he delivers (while in a trance) a monologue to a vole, he begins to construct the ark, which apparently is the very text of the incomplete novel we are reading.

Although *Ararat* might seem less accomplished than the best of his fiction written during the Thirties, it displays several basic traits of Wells's mature artistry. Most appropriate, for example, is the designed incompleteness of its exterior structure, the frustration of any reader expectation of closure. The novel trails off with these final words about the protagonist: "His sentence remains unfinished. The final pages of this story do not appear to be forthcoming. They never may be. As there is so much current interest in it, it has been decided to print and publish the expanding narrative so far as it goes now. So that this is not so much the end as a colophon" (AA, 103; italics deleted). The non-conclusion of this novel makes the reader think about the origins of the book, in a sense returns the reader to the beginning of the story. Such a manner participates in a tradition deriving from Spanish picaresque works like *Don Quixote*, but Wells is discovering it for himself *vis-à-vis* the work of Sterne and Fielding.

The incomplete narrative of *Ararat*, we are told, is *expanding*. In this novel there is no clear starting or finishing point, only an endless round of intensified ebb and flow in an increasingly expanding sea of Noah's mental activity. "Nowhere was there any finality," thinks the protagonist of the novel, who later concludes: "This new-born religion, *this religion of the perpetually increasing and renascent truth,* carries with it an inner compulsion to live, or, if need be, die, as it dictates, directly its apprehension becomes complete. . . . Enquiry replaces dogma. You grow" (AA, 10, 79). *You* speaks to the reader. The use of direct address by Noah and by the narrating anonymous editor of the text finally directs the reader beyond any disappointment with the novel's non-ending to a sense that he or she is to some extent responsible for furthering the story toward closure.

This pattern is reinforced by remarks in the account that draw attention to the reader reading and to the text as artifice. This pattern surfaces, for instance, when we are told that consideration of the "everlasting sequence of the Universe" is "like dealing with an interminable history in an interminable book. You may open the book anywhere; or close it anywhere. This history goes on in spite of you" (AA, 44). The narrative of *Ararat* expands whenever it transgresses its borders as an act of fiction, whenever it splinters its frame by swelling outwards to include the reader within the expanded margin of the text; for just as all of "expanding" history is like a book, so also each reader, as a life in that history, is textually enclosed in a work like *Ararat,* which retells a story from one of the oldest histories, the Bible. Moreover, the narrative of *Ararat* enlarges in the sense that this embracement of the reader, through the splintering frame of the novel, constitutes self-awareness in that reader, an enlargement of the reader's previous range of thought; his realization of personal responsibility is in fact the very mechanism of his inclusion. This reader who experiences the splintering frame of the expanding text, which is also his own expanding thought, will go from the unfinished end of *Ararat* to a reconsideration (as it were, a second reading) of the text of the novel (now transformed through character typology into the text of his or her self). The resultant enlarged insight from this reconsideration comprises one more new start in an interminable human mental evolution of such beginnings. This perception of individual relativity to the whole comprises, as well, the fourth dimension of the novel. Reader and text dialectically interact (as do, in Wells's ideology, the "essential complements" of spirit and matter, freedom and fate). In the process of interacting they mutually develop deeper meaning.

This pattern is reinforced by the novel's protagonist, Noah Lammock, a modern-day "evolved" version of the Old Testament Noah, son of Lamech. Facing World War II, which he consistently images as an inun-

31

dation (AA, 26, 55, 102), Lammock contemplates human destiny. He concludes that mythical stories, historical events, and cardinal personality types in both these stories and events repeat themselves. Even the most elevated artistic vehicles for the transmission of these stories, events and types are repetitive. The "Bible is *the* fundamental book," Lammock observes, "*our* literature is just a footnote to it" (AA, 58). The Bible is, as *Ararat* demonstrates, an inexhaustible sourcebook for mythical, historical and personality types. In a "splintering-frame" remark God specifically cites *The Time Machine* and *The Work, Wealth and Happiness of Mankind* (1932)—the span of Wells's Noah-like career—when he tells Lammock, "*You* have written every book with the idea of a world reconstruction in it for the last hundred years. You may not know it, but you have. Under various names. If you did not actually write it at the time, you absorbed it all. There are too many books now for us to talk about individual authors any more" (AA, 56-57). There is, in short, the type specimen.

There is also a series of variations. So this expression of the Noah-impulse, predominant in certain reappearing personalities like Wells and characteristic of the human collective self, is not static. History expands, as should the aesthetic dimension of each successive literary embodiment of scriptural patterns and the increasingly clarifying insight of each successive embodiment of fundamental personality types. God tells Noah, "History, Sir, has a way of repeating itself—with variations. Always with variations" (AA, 12). Later Lammock echoes this idea (AA, 30)—quite similar to Giovanni Vico's approach to history—eventually realizing that even the concept of God must evolve from the Old Testament notion, through the New Testament image, to the (essentially Romantic) belief that "revolution is the living God" (AA, 70). This belief, in conjunction with the concept of the infinite relativity of human perception, explains the meaning of the gnomic statement in the novel, that "the apprehension of Being is a three-dimensional consciousness system falling through a fourth dimension" (AA, 41). This remark summarizes the reader's ideal experience of "expansion" in the novel.

The "revolution [which] is the living God" refers to a circular repetition and a change, a recurrence with variation. Graphically this pattern may be depicted as a spiral, a three-dimensional locus moving through space around a fixed center at a monotonically increasing or decreasing distance from the center. This spiral pattern, which Wells employed in previous works, echoes Plato's use of the image in *The Republic* as a model of the universe. Principally it likely derives from Wells's familiarity with nineteenth-century astronomical interest in such patterns. A specific source might be Arthur S. Eddington's early twentieth-century treatments of the concept of an expanding universe (explicitly remarked in *Experiment in Autobiography, Babes in the Darkling Wood* and *The Conquest of Time*) and of spiral forms in the universe. In *Stellar Movements and the Structure of the Universe* (1914) Eddington observes: "The form of the arms—a logarithmic spiral—has not as yet given any clue to the dynamics of spiral nebulae. But though we do not understand the cause, we see that there is a widespread law compelling matter to flow in these forms."[40] In the arts, a dialectic of spiral return informs much nineteenth-century Romantic poetry; and interest in this form as a symbol of primitive generation and of human progress—"a pattern of hope"—was expressed just prior to World War I and shortly thereafter by members of the Vorticist movement, including the poet Ezra Pound, the painter Wyndham Lewis, the sculptor Henri Gaudier-Brzaska, and the contributors to the short-lived journal *Blast*, which published T. S. Eliot's "Preludes."[41]

A spiral pattern comprises the emerging inner structure splintering the outer structure of *Ararat*. This spiral pattern, evoked through imagery and complementing the typological (repetitive yet evolving) manner of characterization, vies with the external structure; it expands from within the latter's narrative sequence and its implicit promise of closure or finish. Moreover, it implies two motions. As the intrinsically four-dimensional human mind increasingly clarifies, it expands the circumference of the preceding framework circumscribing that mind's thought; this enlarged ring, as it were, becomes the new framework, which in turn is to be splintered outwardly, and so on *ad infinitum* with no real beginnings or endings. Applied to this capacity of the human mind for "different dimensions of thought" (BB, 72), the spiral pattern endlessly increases its distance from the center. It opens outward into fourth-dimensional possibility as that mind moves through time, or history; this spiral movement of the mind is the expression of spirit paradoxically achieving a fated freedom equivalent to the function of expanded insight in the reader of *Ararat*. The ideal readers of *Ararat* will expand, evolve mentally, as does Noah Lammock, and so will repeat with slight but significant variation basic human personality types.

But as the collective human mind enlarges its metaphorical circumference intellectually, the human race experiences the spiral pattern as a steady diminishment of distance from a mystical center, as a resolution of three-dimensional fragmentation, as a transformation of the fate of matter correspondent to the text of *Ararat*. This text expands in aesthetic value only in terms of the relativity of a reader's broadening perception; it is a self-consuming artifact pointing away from itself to the reader. No Yeatsean widening gyre, Wells's dynamic spiral is another version of his notion of "essential complements," the paradoxical integration of such apparent oppositions as mind (reader) and matter (text), freedom and fate. As the collective human mind expands in its quest for freedom, the fated destiny of the race contracts, for ill or for good. And Ararat, the mountain, objectifies this spiral pattern informing the internal structure of Wells's novel. In its essential configuration a mountain is a spiral, and at the receding distant point of diminishment at the spiral's central axis, at the top of Ararat—the opposite extreme of the increasingly open-ended lower part representing the collective human mind—humanity, as the collective ark (AA, 76), seeks rest and fulfillment. This approach to the summit remains asymptotic, as each "Ark of to-day has to become the world of to-morrow" (AA, 80). Hence Wells's conception of repetition with variation is here expressed by means of an old symbol used with variation; this same concept informs Wells's reliance on evolved character types and on an expanding dynamic (always inconclusive) inner structure splintering the frame of the external structure of *Ararat*.

Twenty-two years earlier, in *The Undying Fire*, Wells reflected a similar view of time without the collateral technique of the splintering frame evoking an aesthetic fourth dimension. In 1934 he referred to this novel as "one of the best pieces of work I ever did. I set great store by it still" (EA, 420). We might wonder why. A dialogue novel, *Fire* retells the biblical story of Job, now a school master whose friends visit him prior to his (successful) operation for cancer and plague him to no avail with numerous challenges to his opinions. Certainly there are skillful passages in this book: Huss's long, energetic polemic on evil in the world demonstrating malignity, carelessness, or mere indifference in creation; the Poesque description—Poe is mentioned—of death in a U-Boat as a metaphor for the human condition. Perhaps it satisfied Wells's early attraction to the theatre, for the novel is dramatic, its manner more like that of a play than of a novel of the time, its dialogue excellent, and its focus on the protagonist's bout with cancer and on a pending operation sufficiently generative of suspense. Also the book advances with admirable clarity Wells's arguments on behalf of education and the development of a "world brain" as crucial to the improvement of humanity's collective will. Each of these contributes a good reason for Wells's high regard for this work. His autobiography provides a clue to still another factor in the book's appeal to its author so late in his career: "in *The Undying Fire*, I was at last fully aware of what I was doing and I took a new line" (EA, 419). Wells treasured this work because it marked an important stage in his developing self-awareness as a thinker and writer, a transition he generally attributed, we should recall, to the year 1920.

This self-awareness infuses the entire book: assessed in its light small details can suddenly radiate meaningful implications. In one minor scene, for instance, Sir Eliphaz, a governor of the school where Job Huss teaches, arrives at the institution and vaguely suffers a slight disorientation: "His eye seemed seeking some point of attachment, and found it at last in the steel engraving of Queen Victoria giving a Bible to a dusky potentate, which adorned the little parlour" (W, 11:82). This trifling gesture indicates authorial disapproval of Eliphaz's standards, recalls Wells's antagonism to the framework of Victorian values and fictional conventions, and points to the biblical source of the novel itself. Departing from his earlier manner, however, Wells does not merely react against what he identifies as the prevailing attitude of his time. In *Fire* he attempts a "new line," the adaptation and advancement of the Old Testament story of Job. Expanding and clarifying the framework of values of this traditional account, the novel becomes a contemporary biblical text; or, in Wells's words, "*The Undying Fire* is that great Hebrew imitation of the Platonic Dialogue, the Book of Job, frankly modernized" (EA, 419). This evolution includes a revision of the religious positions of the biblical Job and his acquaintances, a secularization of theology, and a modification of the protagonist.

Job Huss is a modern version of the human type depicted in the Old Testament Job of Uz. Now both Job's circumstances and his mind have advanced. Huss's core belief is reflected in a letter to him from a former student. "You made us think and feel that the past of the world was our own history; you made us feel that we were in one living story" (W, 11: 167; italics deleted). One living story: *Fire* suggests that every human life manifests a repetition of character types. This view, somewhat Romantic in its intimation of past and present existing in simultaneity,[42] contrasts with the convictions of Mr. Dad, a school governor who asks, "What's history, after all? At the best, it's over and done with" (W, 11: 34). For Wells, not history per se but the human patterns within it are important, patterns obscured by the historian's usual emphasis upon particularization and upon uniqueness of event and participant. Uniqueness is certainly there; so also is the type. Job Huss, then, parallels and at the same time realizes more fully a version of Job of Uz. "Job has become

35

mankind" (W, 11:9): Uz>Huss>Us. And like its protagonist, *Fire* is typical yet unique; it parallels and also advances the biblical story. Whereas *Ararat* fully manifests an aesthetic fourth dimension evoked by the technique of the splintering frame, *Fire*, written just before the onset of Wells's mature literary experimentation, displays no tension between outer and inner structure. It proceeds primarily by means of an innovative development of the original account. Still, its approach to time, as implied in its presentation of evolved character and textual types, anticipates Wells's subsequent interest in fictional structure and an aesthetic fourth dimension.

In light of his creator's reliance upon the typical in text and character in *Fire*, Huss's approach to history as "one living story" also looks forward to Wells's use of the spiral pattern to objectify human evolution or devolution in his later work. Huss intends his concept to refute the human tendency to stress the particular and the unique. To see only these aspects of reality is to be like a person who looks back (or down, if the spiral is conceived of as vertical) from the edge of a tier or circuit of the spiral of human history. Since the degree of gradation is very small, the spiral may appear cylindrical from this perspective, which impression might lead to such cyclical interpretations of history as those of Oswald Spengler. On the other hand, perception of gradation might lead to notions of progress that in effect isolate each time period as complete in identity; this would be especially true of the time-tier of the viewer, which tier might appear distinctive in several aspects from the dreamlike lower concentric rings of history. In Wells's opinion, as we have seen, either impression is mistaken because it is made independently from its essential complement; the larger truth includes uniqueness and typicality (repetition). The trouble is that a look into the spire from any of its circuits fails to disclose how the tiers connect. Furthermore, the viewer cannot see into the forward or upper levels—the future—where dreamlike possibilities exist, even as one in time cannot know heaven, which may be "some other dimension of space, [a] world arranged in planes" (W, 11:94). What is required, and what no person can achieve since no part can know the whole of which it is a part, is an absolute overview. Such a perspective would reveal the entire spiral, near-beginning to near-end, and how each circuit is not only joined to the one preceeding and succeeding it but also in fact exists in perfect continuation with these tiers, is one with them as the locus of developing collective human consciousness moves through time around a fixed mystical center. That fixed center is will.

The Collective Will

Will, a radical concept in Wells's thought and art, is also a significant concern in Victorian fiction. As Victorian fiction develops, it has been suggested, the quality of volition tends to define its characters.[43] Indeed, Jane Eyre in Charlotte Brontë's novel (1847) and Dorothea Brooke in George Eliot's *Middlemarch* (1871-72) learn to exert will in opposition to rigid social norms and, perhaps, in the process demonstrate the belief, as expressed by John Stuart Mill, that education in the broadest sense fulfills will. Eyre and Brooke, however, discover as well the egotism which excessive will can engender, and their example indicates the need to forge a balance between individuality and society. In the case of Eliot, moreover, an adaptation of the Feuerbachian theory of general consciousness in *Middlemarch* hints at something like a Collective Will providing, as it were, a benign Over-Soul for the individual expression of volition. Such a notion is turned on its back, its Schopenhauerian underside thrust up, in the late-Victorian novels of Thomas Hardy.

Like Hardy, Wells also applied a Schopenhauerian understanding of will, most directly very late in his career and then only in modified form. Schopenhauer's influence aside, Wells's interest in will appears in his earliest writings. In Wells's system, the individual will operates in consort with the imagination, which rejects "the thing that is" and inclines toward prophecy. In his fiction both faculties are consistently associated with images of light and fire,[44] for they define for Wells the animating center of human identity. This animating center, as the images also imply, is inherently divine, an early Romantic notion which Wells held to the end of his life and which would not endear him to those of the postwar modern generation who believed they had witnessed the demise of religion and tradition. In *The Undying Fire* Huss shares the biblical Job's belief in "the Will of a God of Light" pervading creation (W, 11: 78). He also revises this belief by identifying this divine Will as the fiery animating principle of the human heart:

> All the brighter shines the flame of God in my heart. If the God in my heart is no son of any heavenly father then he is Prometheus the rebel; it does not shake my faith that he is the Master for whom I will live and die. And all the more do I cling to this fire of human tradition we have lit upon this little planet, if it is the one gleam of spirit in all the windy vastness of a dead and empty universe. (W, 11:80)

Nothing antinomian is implied here, only a sense of the intrinsic divinity of the combined force of individual wills working, as in George Eliot's vision, toward positive collective human purposes. God is the united effort of these wills, of the "concentration of will" that defines "the pattern of the key to master our world and release its imprisoned promise" (EA, 12).

Wells's concept of a Collective Will became most pronounced during the 1930's when he specifically adapted Jungian, Schopenhauerian and Spenglerian ideas in his fiction. Appearing at least as early as *The History of Mr. Polly* the Wellsian version combines a Christian faith in divine providence and pagan trust in natural process. As a radical concept informing Wells's typology of characterization, it fuses a biological emphasis upon the unique and a religious emphasis upon the mystical All. Each individual will is a singular variation within this All, this Collective Will somewhat like Wordsworth's or Emerson's Romantic notion of an Over-Soul. This idea integrates, as essential complements or mutually constitutive oppositions, two notions which intrigued Wells as early as 1891. Then he described how from "the absolute standpoint" natural laws appear to determine the universe inexorably, while from the subjective human standpoint individual effort appears to some extent to shape the future.[45] By 1942 this idea not only recalled Romantic and Jungian notions but also suggested to Wells Einsteinian implications: "From the standpoint of the space-time-continuum there is no movement; the whole system is rigid"; "the four-dimensional universe is rigid, Calvinistic, predestinate; the personal life is not a freedom, though it seems to be a freedom; it is a small subjective pattern of freedom in an unchanging all. There is no conflict between fate and free will" (CT, 84). The Collective Will is similar to an absolute view of human reality, which no individual can know as a whole, though each participates in it. Sometimes Wells's protagonists experience intuitive sensations of this unifying divinelike force comprised of essential complements. They glimpse, in or as if in a dream, other dimensions of human knowledge, other more encompassing planes of human self-awareness, control, and potentiality. They henceforth actively and "freely" will their cooperation with this ultimate benign "fate"—a fate microcosmically reflected in their manifestation of a "typical" personality—like Huss, who feels "summon[ed] . . . to live the residue of his days working and fighting for the unity and release and triumph of mankind" (W, 11:148).

None of Huss's goals are attainable in any ultimate sense. The endless process of expansion underlying his effort is what matters. In struggling against the framework of the current givens of human existence, Huss and others like him press against fate, splintering the frame of its present manifestation. This is freedom, though what is achieved in time is always merely an extension of the "space" within a fate ever circumscribing human destiny. In exercising his unique individual will in this way, Huss conforms to the "typical" or predestining Collective Will. The identity he attains in the process is precisely like that of the Christian saint who renounces self in order to achieve wholeness through voluntary coopera- tion with the divine Will. So freedom is fate, fate freedom—a pivotal paradox or essential complement informing at the most fundamental level Wells's spiral image of time and his coincident employment of a typology of texts and characters.

And it defines his experimentation with fictional structure. In fact it determines the dominance of structure over characterization in his novels. Structure reflects a larger truth for Wells than does individual perception. He agrees with Kant, and those Romantic writers influenced directly or indirectly by Kant, that the human mind creates its own structures and that all forms are descriptions of individual truth. But he converts this fate of subjectivism into its opposite, a freedom insofar as these very structures are transcendentally infused, so that through *time* they com- prise the noumenon, or thing-in-itself, the Collective Will.

Like George Moore, George Gissing, Henry James and Thomas Hardy, Wells turned to the craft of fiction as a response to the dying values of society,[46] but he could never endorse, like Nietzsche, William James, Henri Bergson, Joyce and Woolf, the individual as the standard and source of reality. His attitude agreed with Walter Pater's observation that "modern thought is distinguished from ancient by its cultivation of the 'relative' spirit in place of the 'absolute' ";[47] in contrast to Pater's anxious conclusion, Wells's position never endorsed relativism as a suffi- ciently accurate means of assessing human existence or as an appropriate response to human existence. Beyond Bergsonian *durée*, characterizing each person's experience of time, there exists for Wells the larger relativity of the expanding Collective Will of humanity as it interacts and mysti- cally becomes one with an expanding universe. Just as space and time, in Einstein's theory, comprise a continuum, so do, in Wells's system, Uni- verse and Will; so much so that their identities transpose (in Romantic fashion, perhaps), even as do the unique and the typical, freedom and fate, matter and spirit in Wells's thought. Each of these identities alter- nate with their opposite in the flowing spiral of time, which is the mani- festation of the expanding Collective Will and which constitutes the ever- emerging structure of reality for humanity. Wells's novels, it follows, emphasize structure more than characterization, which consequently is determined by structure in his work. That structure, however, will be expressed as a splintering frame, suggesting both the interaction of life's essential complements and, especially, the eternal emergence of an incomplete potential structure expressing a Collective Will processively evolving from within the present framework. In this way Wells sought to make his art reflect reality.

CHAPTER II

The Cathedral of Ideas

The novels Wells wrote during the Twenties demonstrate his early attempt to subject the "space" of exhausted fictional conventions to the warp of timeliness, or reader relativity, in order to evoke a fourth dimension in his novels. In the early Twenties Wells primarily experimented with "evolved" typical characters and typical texts. In the late Twenties Wells discovered further implications of his use of the technique of the splintering frame—the management of certain fictional conventions in a way designed to frustrate expectations aroused by these conventions; to draw attention to the artificiality of and the ideology behind these conventions; and to point away from the "exhausted" text as a finished artifact and towards the self-aware reader, who participates in the expanded boundary of the text and discovers within himself a dimension for a heightened awareness of and control over human fate. In his novels of the late Twenties Wells used the technique of the splintering frame to intimate the existence of an emergent form evolving within the frame of the novel as well as within the present world mirrored in that novel.[1]

The Early Twenties

Men Like Gods (1923) relates a story about Mr. Barnstaple's attempt at a secret vacation away from an unstimulating job and a domineering wife, and about his accidental transplantation into another dimension manifesting a possible utopian future of Barnstaple's world. The accident, we are told, resolved Barnstaple's uncertainty over the destination of his trip: "it converted the possible answer to Whither? from a fixed and definite place into what mathematicians call ... a locus" (W, 28:9). This very early suggestion in the novel that fixed space may in fact be less definable and confinable than we, of Barnstaple's world, are inclined to imagine is again stressed later in the work when the narrator remarks, "all the peace and fixity that man has ever known or will ever know is but the smoothness of the face of a torrent that flies along with incredible speed from cataract to cataract"; and, he continues, "time was when men could speak of Terra Firma and feel the earth fixed, adamantine

41

beneath their feet. Now they know it whirls through space eddying about a spinning, blindly driven sun amidst a sheeplike drift of stars" (W, 28:255). Matter or space, that is to say, may be comprised of length, breadth and width, but, as Serpentine explains to Barnstaple, it undergoes translation, "which translation [is] in fact duration, through a fourth dimension, *time*" (W, 28:49). Space implies structure, form, order, fixity; time, the fourth dimension, implies the "greater" reality of the inherent and seemingly paradoxical fluidity of spatial fixity.

In *Men Like Gods* Utopia encourages the scientist and the artist equally. Significantly this place is described in terms of books: "it was but one of countless universes that move together in time, that lie against one another, endlessly like the leaves of a book" (W, 28:323; cf. 28:308). Still more pertinent, the Utopians use telepathy rather than words as their primary means of communication. Because of telepathy "they were beautifully unwary in their communications. The ironies, concealments, insincerities, vanities and pretensions of earthly conversation seemed unknown to them. Mr. Barnstaple found this mental nakedness of theirs as sweet and refreshing as the mountain air he was breathing" (W, 28:95-96). Words, Barnstaple comes to realize, are conventional, diachronic forms, seemingly fixed forms too restrictive for higher modes of thought, understanding and communication beyond the current level of his world. When, late in the novel, Barnstaple thinks, "What was the use of words?" (W, 28:307), he expresses Wells's prevalent irritation with the limits of language, specifically with the "uncongenial limitations" of fictional language or convention. Wells desired an ideal telepathic art, but he settled for literary form with a fourth dimension; that is to say, his fiction is comprised of form (the space of literary convention) transformed by the timeliness of its imaginative, prophetic relevance to the reader. The embodiment of this search for a more advanced mode of form discloses an artistic dimension of *Men Like Gods*.

It cannot be satisfactorily argued, I think, that *Men Like Gods* succeeds in meeting Wells's design; the book states rather than renders and resolves the problem. Yet, in reflecting a desire for, as it were, a utopian form the book reveals an artistic sensibility to be more effectively manifested in Wells's subsequent works during the Twenties and particularly during the Thirties when Wells would transform Barnstaple's image of eddying into an objectification of the spiral of time. In *Men Like Gods* Wells tried to broaden the range of fiction by relying on, at least from his point of view, a non-fictional model. *Men Like Gods* represents an evolved version of *Pilgrim's Progress* (1678), replete with typical charac-

42

ters, references to pilgrims visiting Utopia, to a Valley of Rest, to Maidenhead Road in Slough, to Quarantine Crag, and so forth. Wells's novel, like its prototype, begins with a conversion experience. As an evolved text with evolved typical characters, however, Wells's work commences where Bunyan's book ends; for Barnstaple suddenly finds himself transplanted from Slough to Utopia, an edenic, heavenly "world of real happiness and order" (W, 28:225) where he pilgrimlike participates in an educational progress toward self-awareness. Wells manages his adaptation well, even furnishing humorous inversions—for example, having a priest from Barnstaple's world function as Temptation and a person named Serpentine provide illumination. The important feature to observe, however, is Wells's attempt to utilize what he perceived as a non-fictional form or, at least, a model bearing marginally on the genre of fiction in order to transcend the limits of the novel of his day. Adapting Bunyan's work permitted the preservation of the free episodic manner favored by Wells and, at the same time, provided a didactic vehicle, attendant with certain audience expectations, by means of which Wells tried to move beyond the confining forms of fictional conventions. In a sense Wells saw Bunyan's allegorical model (albeit conventional in its kind) as at once timeless and timely, as a work with an adaptable form able to involve the reader in a "timely" prophetic message about a "higher" reality (as it were, a fourth dimension) for the human self.

In his next novel, *The Dream* (1924), Wells sought to wed the dialogue novel with which he had experimented earlier and a very commonplace plot. By fashioning a narrative frame disparate from that usually associated with the essentially Victorian story presented within the frame, Wells apparently intended to create an incongruity dramatizing the inadequacy of current fiction as well as of the current mode of human existence it both reflected and reinforced. *The Dream* is a novel of antipodes tenuously held together in dynamic tension. Early in the novel, Sarnac, the Utopian citizen narrating his dream of having lived centuries ago in the Days of Confusion (*The Dream* is *Men Like Gods* told from the other side), indicates a central bifurcation in the work when he says, "I am still half Harry Mortimer Smith and only half myself. I am still only in memory but half in feeling also that young English barbarian in the Age of Confusion. And yet all the time I am looking at my story from our point of view and telling it in Sarnac's voice" (W, 28:418). A tension, in short, exists between the realm of sensation or the past (the plot of the novel) and the realm of mind or the future (the frame of the novel).

43

The disparity between Sarnac's enlightened voice (the frame) and Smith's muddled life (the story) surfaces whenever the novel alternates, without transition, between a straightforward seriousness and an undercutting satiric tone. This tension persists in various ways until the very conclusion of the work, where the reader's sense of reality, of comfort, is assaulted one last time when Sarnac asserts, "It was a life . . . and it was a dream, a dream within this life; and this life too is a dream (W, 28: 653). Throughout the novel the apparently fixed nature of the story (Smith's life) is made uncertain by the influx of the fourth dimension (Sarnac's Utopia); as its coordinates lose specified fixity in space, the reality of the plot is transformed into the "greater" reality of a story unmoored by and seen through time.

The Dream was designed to counter the type of novels Wells thought prevailed during the early part of the twentieth century, novels telling "people what their minds were prepared to receive, searching for what [they] should tell rather in the mind and expectation of the hearer or reader—who was the person who paid—than in the unendowed wildernesses of reality. . . . the popular literature of the age in which Harry Mortimer Smith was living was more abundant, more cynically insincere, lazy, cheap and empty than anything that the world had ever seen before" (W, 28:529-530). Arthur Conan Doyle typifies a related problem, Sarnac explains, for his "stories had little psychology in them; he tangled a skein of clews in order to disentangle it again, and his readers forgot the interest of the problem in the interest of the puzzle" (W, 28:531). Even though a puzzle is unfolded in Sarnac's narrative, *The Dream* never loses sight of the problem because the frame of the puzzle (Sarnac's voice) vies with the story (Smith's life) for our attention; and as a consequence of this early manifestation of Wells's splintering frame technique the reader becomes, as it were, a self-conscious eavesdropper listening to a narrative disclosed piecemeal yet narratively framed for a Utopian audience appreciative of a greater sense (as it were, the fourth dimension) of reality than we are capable of apprehending.

The artistic management of tension or bifurcation in *The Dream* keeps the puzzle intimately related to the problem; it keeps the context immediately related to the frame even while that context vies with the frame, just as reality and dream become for Sarnac as interwoven as space and time. The fourth dimension of *The Dream* emanates from the reader's experience of the novel's dialectical concern with the antagonism as well as the paradoxically organic relation between fixity and fluidity, past and future, space and time, reality and dream, story and frame—all embedded in an account, vacillating between earnestness and satire, by a narrator divided between memories based on sensation and perceptions based on reason.

In *Christina Alberta's Father* (1925) Wells's search for an appropriate fictional structure resulted in a similar, if somewhat more advanced strategy. In this work the omniscient narrator intrudes in mood-breaking ways, deliberately drawing attention to himself so as to splinter the narrative frame, to weaken the reader's confidence in the narrator's control, and to prevent the reader from comfortably submerging himself into the mere story of Albert Preemby's belief he is Sargon reborn and of Christina's development of self-awareness. A telling intrusion occurs at the opening of the second chapter, when the narrator entreats us to trust him and to fathom the problems subverting his effort to write the novel: "This story, it was clearly explained in the first paragraph of the first chapter, is a story about Mr. Preemby. . . . That statement has all the value of an ordinary commercial guarantee, and on no account shall we ever wander far from Mr. Preemby" (CA, 28). Nevertheless, the narrator confesses, Preemby's daughter plays an important part in the story, "and even after it has begun, and while it goes on, and right up to the end, Christina Alberta will continue to intrude" (CA, 28). This problem emerges frequently in the work, for instance when we are again reminded that "Christina Alberta has got herself hatched into this story much like a young cuckoo in a wagtail's nest and it is impossible to ignore her" (CA, 59). By recurrent suggestions that he is not in control, the narrator disintegrates the very trust he pretends to guarantee and dispels the fictional illusion usually enjoyed by the engaged reader.

As a device in Wells's technique of the splintering frame, the narrative voice enters and distorts the picture, resulting in the reader's uncomfortable self-awareness of the fact that he is reading a work of fiction by an author who is uncomfortably self-conscious; and this self-awareness is stimulated in order to replace the reader's normal expectations and his usual passive disposition while reading with an active engagement, without illusion, in deriving the *meaning* (i.e., experiencing the *duration*) of the story. The fundamental dilemma with which the narrator and the reader must cope, the tug of war between Christina and Preemby, is reflected in the title of the novel, which announces Preemby as the central focus but which attributes identity to him only as Christina's father; and so Christina has challenged Preemby even for the title of *his* book. This sort of self-conscious intrusion upon the conventional perimeter of the novel, reminiscent of Sterne and Fielding, demonstrates Wells's discontent with the formulae of the post-Victorian novel and his conscious artistic inventiveness. It also anticipates Wells's later conversion (with Hegelian implications) of his search for form into a dynamic mode of potential structure which is not fixed but is four-dimensional in that it exists only *in the process* of emerging relative to the reader's perception of it.

As the narrator's difficulty with them suggests, Christina and Preemby appear to serve as opposing "typical" forces, even biblically typical. Believing himself to be an "advanced" reincarnation of Sargon, Preemby sets out Christlike to become "the new Saviour of mankind," to reveal that this "life is full of meaning and order" (CA, 190, 231). Like an Anti-Christ, Christina, whose irreligious, amoral, anti-social mind is "entirely swept and void of positive and restraining convictions," behaves as "the Ultimate Modern Girl," as "a sceptic, an ally of the Anti-Power" (CA, 60, 134, 235). Initially she relishes total freedom from parental control: "the discretions and scruples of others were not for her. She had seen no reason for their prudent hesitations, their conventions and restraints" (CA, 245). In fact, as we later learn, she is not Preemby's child but the daughter of Mrs. Preemby and Dr. Devizes, a disclosure which makes the novel's title even more enigmatic.

As in *The Dream*, apparent antagonism in *Christina Alberta's Father* actually points to a potential unity, coherence or synthesis in the natural scheme of things. This implication certainly informs Mr. Preemby's role as an evolved antitype for Sargon and Christ, former antitypes now reduced to types. In the sensuous three-dimensional reality of space, "the primary self"—the "instinctive, individual, fearful, greedy, lustful, jealous, self-assertive" features of humanity (CA, 290)—rages rampantly. Because of her youth, Christina lives primarily in space, a creature of the senses and oblivious to time. Her legal father, in contrast, lives in his mind, where he thinks he is Sargon, and believes he travels in time rather than through space (CA, 177). Preemby experiences the fourth dimension of reality, space undergoing duration, where "the social self" can emerge and stress "social instincts and dispositions arising out of family life" (CA, 290). Because each is polarized, Christina and Preemby seem antagonistic; together they represent a bifurcation defining the human psyche, which integrates these two components of the self through some mysterious means beyond human knowledge. Everyone is "a creature in a state of internal conflict, quicker, fiercer mortal instincts at issue with a deeper, calmer, less brightly lit, but finally stronger drive towards immortal purposes" (CA, 290). This observation explains the meaning of Preemby's belief that Sargon's blood flows through everyone's veins, that we all descend from Sargon and so are all kings—hence it does not matter who in actuality is Christina's father; and it underscores Christina's education away from total concern with her "primary self" toward awareness of her "social self" and of the capacity of the human race to evolve "towards synthesis and co-operation" (CA, 384).

Of the many strategies Wells employs to subvert reader expectations as elicited by the formulae of fictional conventions, the most accomplished, in terms of his search for structure, appears at the end of the novel. The final pages of the book focus on Robert Roothing, who has been trying to write a novel throughout the course of Wells's novel. Ruthing ruminates on Preemby's death: "It was as though an interesting story had come to an abrupt end in the middle, as though all its concluding chapters had been torn out rudely and unreasonably" (CA, 365). After one final effort Roothing decides to abandon his novel, for he, like Barnstaple in *Men Like Gods*, wonders about the limits of language, especially since "there is only the world that has been and a world that is to be" (CA, 400); that is to say, there is (in implied Hegelian fashion) only process, space warped by time, and so no meaningful form (fixed space or fictional convention) is feasible. Wells metamorphoses this very dilemma into a tentative resolution or synthesis. By ending his novel with Roothing's decision to abort a novel, Wells conveys an approximate sense of a conclusion without really ending. Covertly, Roothing's failure points to Wells's deliberate refusal to resolve numerous loose ends in the novel (e.g., Christina's presumably pending marriage); and Roothing's inability to finish his work provides another loose end paradoxically serving as a tentative climax for Wells's novel, which thereby has transcended the limited expectations of readers inured to fictional conventions.

In fiction, we are told in Wells's novel, "the love story, the treasure story, the career, getting on, making a fortune, the personal deed and victory, the sacrifices for an individual friend or love or leader ... [remain] no longer the whole of life and sometimes not even the leading interest in life" (CA, 385). Indeed *Christina Alberta's Father* denies the reader the comfort of identifying fully with any of these themes, not only by frustrating expectations of a conventional conclusion but from the outset by presenting an intrusive narrator who dispels the reader's illusion of reality and never permits him to become so absorbed in the "puzzle" that he loses sight of the "problem." The reader must, as it were, aid the narrator in the construction of the novel or, at least, consciously share in the problems related to the process of writing it; and the tentative ending, objectified in Roothing's abandonment of his book, provides a last instance of

47

how the reader enters the picture through the splintering frame. In a sense the reader is invited to finish the novel, to attain a more satisfying synthesis in the novel, in his life, and in himself (comprised of seemingly antagonistic "primary" and "social" selves); for finally whenever the narrative frame gets into the picture, the distinction between reality and fiction (dream), between life and art, dissolves. Like Roothing, who became involved in Preemby's "sacrifice," puts his writing aside at the end and goes outside, we are invited to move the novel toward a still more synthetic completion by living our lives in society, by contributing to Christina's eventually conscious effort to bring about a greater social synthesis.

Wells maintained, as we noted, that art should follow life, which "is diversity and entertainment, not completion and satisfaction." *Christina Alberta's Father* is a superb realization of Wells's view of the relation between art and life, of how art is drawn from life, progresses toward but ideally never achieves fixed form, as it in-structs and instructs the reader *on* by involving him *in* the question of how to live. Even as Preemby dies yet his Sargon spirit is said to be reborn eternally, so too the emergent structure of Wells's book expires prematurely, yet its "typical" spirit or timely/timeless principle of animation ideally revives eternally within readers and finds expression in their subsequent life. In striving for structure without achieving it, in paradoxically converting the search for form into a tentative emergent form, *Christina Alberta's Father* transforms fictional space (the form of literary convention) by existing also in time; its developing structure in-forms within the text and finally within the reader, who enters the picture through the splintering frame and whose actual life can bring the novel to a more synthetic conclusion. This inclusion of the reader's relative potentiality for action manifests the novel's fourth dimension.

The Late Twenties

Clearly Wells's manner exemplifies a characteristic of dialectical thought, that characteristic whereby, according to Frederic Jameson, "the older mental operation or problem-solving [is placed] in a new and larger context . . . convert[ing] the problem itself into a solution."[2] That Wells was conscious of the dialectical feature of his experiments with structure is suggested in *The World of William Clissold: A Novel at a New Angle* (1926), in which Hegelian notions are discussed directly, if somewhat inaccurately. In this novel Clissold claims to modify the Hegelian doctrine "which tells us that the Thing-that-is is always shattered at last to make way for a higher synthesis by the Thing-that-it-isn't," to include "the triangularity of human affairs" (WC, 170, 329); this triangularity is comprised of conservative forces, liberal energy, and creative spirit (or, we might say, of thesis, antithesis, and catalyst). This novel represents Wells's attempt to depict the new interrelationship prophesied in *Christina Alberta's Father*, to convey aesthetically the interaction of space and time in a "synthesis . . . replacing the scattered autonomous various individualism of the past by a more and more intricate inter-dependent life" (WC, 253). This aim underlies the journal format of Clissold's narrative, which intermingles as inextricably as possible the personal details of his life and the political movements, economic forces and social developments of his time. As a *Novel at a New Angle*, the work is designed to assault a reader's expectations, particularly anticipation of his conventional accommodation by the narrator and relaxed involvement in the illusion of the story. Even the reader's likely objections are anticipated, for instance, when Clementina enters Clissold's study, peripherally reviews what he has written so far, and complains that she expected to read something engaging about him rather than something dull about -*isms*. Clissold irritably dismisses her and then explains to *us* that no digressions appear in his narrative because the true account of his or of any life must include the story of humanity—biography and autobiography become history; the novelist becomes journalist.

Clissold stresses human progress toward the "synthetic and comprehensive" (WC, 88), and his narrative, mimetic of this ongoing development, lacks structure or, more accurately, takes on vague in-forming/informing shape as his discussion unfolds. Admitting uncertainty as to how to get his book underway, Clissold confesses at one point that he has been "beating about the bush for five sections"; he wonders, consequently, if life's show has any plot and he suspects that we all must improvise a part (WC, 42-43). Finally, however, Clissold asserts a faith in an order latent in the scheme of things and in all improvised parts; and his narrative reflects his search for an order or a structure to define and to embody his life's reality as it is manifested in "time and space" (WC, 28). The search is crucial for him: "My mind seeks it and needs it; the spectacle remains incoherent in spite of all my seeking" (WC, 43). The prevalent notions of order prove insufficient for Clissold, who believes that forms are simultaneously necessary and restrictive. Space, he is sure, is not "a framework of three dimensions as rectangular as a window sash": for, as Einstein explained, through time or the fourth dimension

49

"space is bent in some incomprehensible fashion" so that finally space provides "possibly unstable co-ordinates" (WC, 52).

Clissold's account, it follows, tries to avoid the misleading spatial co-ordinates of conventional fiction. Because the order underlying the universe remains beyond current human comprehension, Clissold's narrative apprehends this order aesthetically as a potentiality of reality. That "there is order in the universe" (WC, 48) is objectified in the novel by the window out of which Clissold frequently looks. When the book commences—the first section is entitled "The Frame of the Picture"—it is November, and so the window is closed. Later in the work Spring arrives, and the window is opened; this change suggests at that point in the novel Clissold's realization that "that frame of [the] world" presents an order open to the fluidity of time. That flux is universal comprises a refrain in the novel, but the cyclical passing of the seasons accompanied by the evolution of Clissold's thought implies that in some sense flux is contained, even as the notion of Spring seems framed by the window's sides. So too the narrative frame, such as it is, of Clissold's story is "opened" to exhibit an emerging order characterized by timeliness, by its relativity to the reader. The narrative frame, like the window and the seasons, provides structure, but this structure is open to expansion from the flux of particulars within it.

Two explicit instances of the technique of splintering the frame, at the level of narrative voice, and of the related violation of reader expectation occur when Clissold thinks, "I may have been created even as I write here, created with the illusion of past memories in my mind. Or the reader may have come into being in the very act of reading this sentence"; and when he refers directly to Wells, "if a character may for once turn on his creator and be frank about him" (WC, 78, 627). At such moments the engaged reader loses the illusion usually engendered by a fictional text and he becomes self-conscious of his role as a reader. By asserting his emancipation from his creator and thereby surprising the reader into self-awareness, Clissold transcends the Jamesian boundaries separating life and art, fact and fiction—which is to say finally that the reader is forced "into being" at some level of his perception so as to question "the thing that is" and perhaps to see beyond the limits of the conventional three-dimensionality of the windowlike fictional frame or of the windowlike frame of his daily life.

Such blurring of "spatial" distinctions, in life as well as in fiction, is a feature of the "timely" aesthetic dimension of Clissold's "living art" (WC, 672) aspiring toward greater synthesis. His artistry contrasts with that of Clementina, whose emphasis on the distinctive self rather than on the social or synthetic self compels her to stifle her latent creativity within (ironically) the prescribed limits of extant poetic forms: "she will not even look at the *framework* in which such things are set and which is continually affecting and determining such things" (WC, 194; italics added). Clissold hopes his narrative will serve as a "catalytic agent" (WC, 770) among conservative and liberal forces, as an expression of catalytic creative will contributing to human awareness (relativity) and to the realization of four-dimensionality in life and in art; and, appropriately, the book ends without a conclusion (WC, 756, 781, 786). Clissold dies before he completes his work, and his brother, who serves as the reader's surrogate, suggests in an epilogue how he and we must "come into being" or awaken to the complex dimensionality of our lives so as to provide, through our thoughts and actions, the *living* completion, the fourth dimension, to the "living art" of Clissold's book.

Wells's experimentation with fictional structure and his development of a tentative, evolving structure also characterize *Meanwhile: The Picture of a Lady* (1927), the subtitle of which invites speculation about the book's relation to James's *Portrait of a Lady* (1881, 1908). A careful comparison of the two works would yield a fascinating study—Wells actually rewrites certain scenes from James's novel—but for our immediate purposes the important observations to make are that his controversy with James still weighed heavily upon Wells's mind in the late Twenties and that this continued sensitivity reinforces an argument for Wells's artistic self-consciousness during this period. Apparently his controversy with James and his drive to demonstrate alternative fictional modes inform Wells's novels during the Twenties, and even in his autobiography the debate with James finds a prominent place.

In *Meanwhile* Wells refuses to provide a nicely framed *portrait*, with an emphasis on completion or finish (*forma formata*) arrived at arbitrarily through (in his opinion) the artist's egocentric, subjective selectivity of detail; rather, he presents a *picture*, the frame of which (like that of Clissold's window) does not confine or determine the art work and the subject of which concerns human life in all its photographic reality—including its confusions, its seemingly unaesthetic clutter, and its inclusiveness. Pictures, in Wells's opinion, are a higher mode of art than are portraits because they transcend the individual egocentricity of the artist, who tyranically seeks to control the flux of real human experience; pictures only suggest the inherent potential order beneath human exis-

51

tence, convey intimations of this latent order aesthetically in an apparent formlessness evolving into form (*forma formans*).

Meanwhile describes the burgeoning awareness, in Cynthia and Philip Ryland (wealthy English citizens living in Italy), of their responsibility for other people. Through the catalytic agency of Sempak, who speaks of Einstein's theories about time, the Rylands try to resolve their marital difficulties and, as well, slowly discover their involvement in the English coal-miner's strike and in the rise of Italian Fascism, both described as a civil war (M, 153, 164). All three of these thematic concerns coalesce to objectify the divided nature of or civil war within the human self, and the drama of the novel actually centers on this internal division. But (in Hegelian fashion) latent in the split is its own resolution, with the result that Cynthia's spirituality and Philip's materialism are held together by Sempak's catalytic, integrating mind or will; so that together they demonstrate the triangularity of human relations stressed in *Christina Alberta's Father* and *The World of William Clissold*.

. These three characters partake of a fluid, drifting relationship, and appropriately the novel about them conveys an impression of formlessness. When Sempak, who delights in the wild African-looking (*picture*) edge of the meticulous (*portrait*) gardens on the Rylands' Italian estate, expresses his doubt that "life has very much use for a perfect thing, for finished grace and beauty, than an artist for his last year's masterpiece" (M, 83), he touches on an aesthetic principle informing *Meanwhile*. This principle is most evident in the dialogue of the novel, for the open-ended and freely-flowing dialogue serves Wells as an aesthetic device including at once a wildness akin to the African-looking part of the estate and an incomprehensible, inherent direction and order. The naturalness of conversation and its intrinsic emerging order or structure are implied when Cynthia contemplates some palm trees: "Each frond curved over to its end harmoniously and evenly, so that to follow it was like hearing a long cadence, and the leaflets stood up at the curve and then slanted and each was just the least bit in the world smaller and slanted the fraction of an inch more steeply than the one below it. . . . Each played a witty variation on the common theme" (M, 157-158). Nature, for Wells as for Hegel, and human speech simultaneously emphasize individual detail and the place of each unique detail in a transcendent whole.

Underlying the frond passage is Wells's notion of Gothic architecture. Very early in the novel a conversation is described as "a cathedral of ideas. A Gothic cathedral. Everything said had a sort of freedom and yet everything belonged" (M, 23-24). That this style of architecture exemplifies natural or organic artistry is remarked later in the novel when Cynthia describes a steep hillside: "It streams up and up and up, and over it brood the wet black precipices of the mountains, endlessly vertical. . . . It is like all the Gothic in the world multipled by ten. It is like listening to some tremendous crescendo" (M, 175). *Meanwhile* is, in these terms, Gothic—a cluster of individual, seemingly incongruous matters held together by some nearly perceptible order of internal relationship.

The novel, like Philip's writing project, "seem[s] to begin at half a dozen places and it is only after a time that one finds that this joins up with that" (M, 196). They *do* join. *Meanwhile* abounds in fragments: parts of letters, incomplete journal entries, sentences recalled out of context, random thoughts, partial conversations, loose sheets of paper covered with "disconnected sentences" (M, 226). At this or that point, however, the fragments relate, even as unique human individuals belong collectively to a race progressing (in Wells's view) toward unification. The seemingly inchoate fragments of *Meanwhile* actually contribute to a central development: the awakening of the Rylands in regard to themselves (as individuals and as spouses), to their country, and to mankind. The elements of the novel's outer structural disorder collectively convey an aesthetic sense of an elusive, pervading order; and appropriately, at the end of the novel Cynthia, seeing beneath the surface of her husband's infidelity (which parallels the striking miners' alleged infidelity to their country), undergoes a mystical experience revealing a transcendent organizing force in herself and in all of humanity. In short, the "hotchpotch of ideas" (M, 253) constituting the seemingly plotless material of *Meanwhile* builds, as it were, vertically toward a mystical awareness, toward a crescendo similar to that intimated by the Gothic-looking mountain contemplated by Cynthia.

The aesthetic achievement of *Meanwhile* derives from Wells's attempt to create a literary equivalent to his conception of Gothic architecture. This technique recalls similar efforts by Hardy in *Jude the Obscure* and by Lawrence in *The Rainbow* (1915); and it replies specifically to James's idea of Gothic in *The Portrait of a Lady*, though in fact this novel conforms to James's "prefer[ence for] the 'square,' the 'regular,' the 'well-proportioned' Palladian styles as analogue for the construction of his fiction."[3] The appropriateness of the analogy for *Meanwhile* becomes evident when Gothic form is perceived as a molding of space evolving as a temporal experience, as an unrigid form always unfinished and in motion, forever in the act of becoming.[4] Like a Gothic edifice, *Meanwhile* combines fragments (of thoughts, conversations and letters) as unique yet organically related variations on a theme; and like a Gothic edifice, *Meanwhile* evinces a growing developing design, space undergoing time, inner structural form in the act of evolving into being. The novel, consequently, remains incomplete, an untidy picture rather than a finished portrait. The implied inclusion of the reader in this picture intensifies this lack of perfection: "There must be thousands of people . . . who needed only sufficient stimulation to be released in this fashion from the sort of verbal anchylosis that had kept [Philip] inexpressive" (M, 298). The reader, it follows, should add his expression to the developing Gothic-like "cathedral of ideas" emerging in the novel, the inner structure of which avoids the fixed and confining three-dimensionality of external structures of the sort evident in portraits. This internal structure remains latent even as it continually evolves, without final resolution, through a mysterious integration of the fragments of human temporal reality; it also remains latent because each reader has yet to provide his own unique variation on the theme implicit in this emergent inner structural principle. As we have seen in other novels he wrote during the Twenties, this "timely" inclusion of the reader's relativity is a direct result of Wells's technique of splintering the frame of a novel (a *portrait* of fixed space) to achieve a fourth dimension in his fiction (a *picture* of space in time).

Concern with fictional structure also characterizes *Mr. Blettsworthy on Rampole Island* (1928), which in later years Wells referred to as "another breach of established literary standards with which, in spite of its very tepid reception, I am mainly content" (EA, 421-422). This novel relates how Blettsworthy is shipwrecked and then captured by a tribe of cannibals on an island allegorically representing England during the Twenties. The novel abounds in echoes from and revisions of Voltaire's *Candide* (1759), Melville's *Moby-Dick* (1851), Conrad's fiction and, among others, possibly Ford's *The Good Soldier* (1915). Whatever expectations these echoes generate in the reader are deliberately violated in this novel departing from "established literary standards."

Central to Wells's manner of reversing conventional expectations is the interjection, into the novel's first-person narrative, of modes of writing generally (even if erroneously) considered quite outside the normal perimeter of fictional form. Midway in the book, for example, appears a very long natural history of the Giant Sloth; the manner of the passage derives from scientific and anthropological treatises (here thinly disguising an allegory on the inertia of all human institutions), and it is so dissonant to the narrative technique preceding it that the reader is, as it were, shocked out of any complacently passive or vicarious immersion in the fictive illusion of the story. This "shock" is designed to awaken the reader to the serious "problem" beyond the immediate "puzzle" of the story as well as to the relative significance of this problem to the reader.

This dislocation in the narrative is adumbrated and succeeded by another fragmenting device, the recurrent instances of amnesia (followed by "awakenings") in the narrator, who indicates from the first that he would like "to subordinate reality to a gracious and ample use of language" (portrait) but that he is "divided against [him]self" and so cannot prevent "great disconnected portions of [him]self" from intruding (picture) (MB, 6-7). Blettsworthy is divided between his paternally inherited practical side, which prefers form or order, and his maternally inherited inquisitive side, which prefers unrestricted freedom; and this problem affects him as a writer, for he finds "the technical ingenuities required hampered [his] creative impulse" (MB, 36). No wonder, then, that Blettsworthy "warn[s] the reader plainly" that a "certain obscurity and disconnectedness," a "disarrangement of the order of these events in time" characterize his narrative (MB, 161). Indeed, his account of how amnesia-inducing accidents undermine his sense of "completest confidence in [him]self, mankind and nature" is told so "disjointedly and amorphously" that the reader's confidence in the details or "the surface of things" in the narrative is shaken and his cognitive processes provoked by the need to derive his own meaning and order from the obscurity and disconnectedness of the account (MB, 101-102, 105).

As a novel, *Rampole Island* is at war with itself, its external or surface structure (reinforced by echoes from other works) always under assault by some internal force. Implicit throughout the novel is an attack on deceptively superficial fictional conventions. When Blettsworthy at one point during his misadventures cries out, "My God! ... this isn't like they do it in books" (MB, 244), he really expresses Wells's repudiation of those fictional conventions which convey a false sense of order. As in *Tono-Bungay*, something more "formless and indefinite" (MB, 266), something more existential lies beneath the seeming solidity of forms in society and in art. Appropriately, the reader finds himself adrift in the novel, even as Blettsworthy floats aimlessly for an indefinite period on the sea (a metaphor for change within formlessness [MB, 154]). In this respect *Rampole Island* is an anti-novel; it turns on itself by frustrating normal reader expectations during the Twenties in order to reveal "the real world looming through the mists of ... [readers'] illusions" (MB, 268), illusions resulting in and reinforced by pernicious fictional conven-

55

tions. In turning upon itself, it draws attention to the artifice of these conventions and finally points away from itself and towards the reader, who must provide the meaning of the account. The dislocations resulting from Wells's technique of the splintering frame in this novel are designed to awaken the reader out of a trancelike amnesia, out of an illusory fictionlike existence, through "wakeful hours," to a *developing* awareness (similar to Barnstaple's in *Men Like Gods* and the Rylands' in *Meanwhile*) that "the whole universe, and [the reader] with it, had become something different, as if the self [he] had known hitherto had been a dream in a dream world, and this now was reality" (MB, 52).

Just as Blettsworthy is divided against himself yet progresses toward (albeit not achieving) synthetic self-awareness and just as the reader is alienated by the narrative but also involved in it, the novel remains formless while it imparts a sense of emerging form from within. The novel plays antithesis to its own thesis. Its developing latent synthesis reflects Wells's sense of the formlessness of the human mind which nonetheless possesses a potentiality for form, a capacity to evolve in time; for in the sealike rhythm of time "between waking and sleep . . . nearly imperceptible distinctions open to abysmal depth, and contrariwise the most disconnected things assume an air of close analogy and vivid logicality" (MB, 207). The fragmentation of outer structure which somehow (in Hegelian manner) provides the basis for an emergent synthetic form as well as the inclusion of the reader as an agent of this evolving process define the "timely," or fourth, dimension of *Rampole Island*, a novel in which the "space" of fictional conventions undergoes the warp of timeliness, as if in it "some sudden twist of time and space" has occurred (MB, 165) not only for Blettsworthy but for us as well.

In 1929, Wells published *The King Who Was a King: The Book of a Film*, and although its American edition bore the subtitle *An Unconventional Novel*, in fact the work is not a novel. Even if the filmscript dramatizes Wells's discomfort with the limits of fictional modes, even if it exhibits a use of *montage* which coalesces moments in time and events in space in such a manner that space is made fluid, the book proves to be terribly disappointing as a whole. Nevertheless, this experiment did not signal the decline of Wells's inventiveness in creatively managing fictional structure. During the next decade Wells continued to protest the restraints of fictional formulae as well as, through his technique of the splintering frame, to strive for a fourth dimension in his own work. The novels of the Thirties, at least some of them, represent the crowning achievement of Wells's career as a writer. The aesthetic attainment, however, proceeds from Wells's self-conscious management during the Twenties of an in-forming structure, which he saw as a Gothic cathedral of ideas—a beautiful, mystical, and potential form (*forma formans*) in the process of evolving within the frame of a novel as well as within the present world mirrored in that novel.

CHAPTER III

The Multidimensional Framework
of the Mind

During the Thirties Wells's experiment with fictional structure reached its apogee. Not every novel he published during this decade is of equal merit, as his sometimes disappointing engagements with the *Bildungsroman* reveal. Viewed collectively, however, and scrutinized selectively in depth, the fiction he wrote during the Thirties hardly conveys an impression of casualness in its manner or in its effect. These novels comprise an accomplished modern development of the turn-of-the-century emphasis on structure in the novel. They represent the maturation and rich achievement of the artistic consciousness evident in Wells's fiction of the preceding decade. Moreover, they demonstrate better than ever before in his work the compatibility of ideas and art.

Lost Places in Dreams and Texts

However much *The Autocracy of Mr. Parham* (1930) still amused its author several years after its appearance, Wells readily admitted that few people shared his enthusiasm for this "boisterous caricature" (EA, 421) of a chauvinistic academic who blindly adheres to English tradition and who during a séance has a dream in which a Master Spirit from Mars invades his body and transforms him into a fascist dictator.[1] The story of Parham, an it-can-happen-here book, details the stages of the establishment of this English dictatorship. Much of the book's humor has paled with the years, and critics of Wells's work have either ignored this novel entirely or dismissed it in passing. Whatever its shortcomings, however, its appearance at a critical juncture between the two most significant decades in Wells's literary career suggests that we ought to be sensitive to its adumbration of a more mature expression of Wells's revisionary cast of mind and of his concomitant experimentation with fictional structure and typical characterization. Especially noteworthy is its manifestation of Wells's developing mastery of a fictional technique suitable to both his social and his artistic aims, in this instance his use of a fictional manner derived from a revision of Petronius' *Satyricon*.

Parham is an historian interested in Cardinal Richelieu, the seventeenth-century French nationalist who advocated centralized royal authority. Parham's story abounds in allusions to historical figures, often presented in sequences suggestive of a repetition through time of certain personality types. To be sure, any implied parallelism between Parham and Sargon, Alexander the Great, Genghis Khan, Julius Caesar, and Napoleon Bonaparte is parodic; but within this rather obvious humor lies a more covert point about the readiness of people (in Wells's opinion) to relate to history as if it were circularly self-defined, fixed, and dependent on monolithically recurrent personality types. Parham, whose classical education encourages him to "lose all sense of current events" and to "get such history as [he has] swallowed repeating itself" (AP, 28), displays this very tendency. He fears that the rising generation fails to perceive the continuity of history and that, consequently, "round and about the present appearances of historical continuity something else quite different and novel and not so much menacing as dematerializing these appearances was happening" (AP, 9). Appropriately, during his dream of his dictatorship, Parham believes his mission to include the reassertion of history. For him "it is the past that rules; it is the past that points us on to our assured Destinies" (AP, 190). Responding (in his dream) to his view of the world "going through a phase of moral and intellectual disintegration; its bonds relaxed; its definite lines crumbled" (AP, 68), he undertakes a mission "to make history and to make it larger and heavier and with a greater displacement of the fluidities of life than it had ever been made before" (AP, 167).

Ironical is the fact that Parham's belief finds embodiment in a dream, for such a belief is (in Wells's view) a delusion akin to any dream. Moreover, as the novels Wells wrote during the Twenties make abundantly evident, a dreamlike fluidity with "definite lines crumbled" characterizes human life. Time is fluid, or relative, Wells makes clear, and as a result every period of history comprises a mere phase in an apparently infinite series of alternate possibilities, or dimensions. Each phase shares something essential with any other phase, but it also differs to some significant degree—as if each were related but not quite identical dreams within some larger dream-context. Pertinently, at the end of the novel we learn that Parham and Sir Bussy Woodcock have experienced in precisely the same period of time, "a similar dream," though "not exactly the same dream" (AP, 323).

59

What is true for Wells about historical events and human experience generally is, as we have seen elsewhere, applicable to personality types appearing in the past and in the present. *Parham* is a novel populated by caricatures rather than by three-dimensional characters, a manner reflecting Wells's artistic intention to present personages at once unique and typical. Expanding upon the view of time expressed in the novels he wrote during the Twenties, Wells now began to think of time as a polymorphous dimensionality including various unique species evolving towards an ideal mode of being. This ideal mode is implicit in the essential typicality underlying all uniqueness, a paradoxical state permitting a variety of alternate possibilities for humanity, which at any given moment lives as if in a dream.[2] Event and character, then, are at once repetitious and unique; like the dream shared by Parham and Woodcock, historical events and human types are throughout time similar without being precisely identical.

And what is true for Wells about historical events and personality types is, as even *Men Like Gods* implies, equally true about art works. Like events and like individuals, literary texts incorporate a unique and a typical identity. Herein lies the significance of Parham's reference to Petronious' *Satyricon* (AP, 46-47). *Parham*, especially the first half, is designed to echo the manner of the *Satyricon*, though this act of imitation finally duplicates the Classical work only slightly. Like Petronius' work (which survives in fragments), Wells's book exhibits a loosely organized satirical plot permitting frequent digressions, and emphasizes (through Parham's "refined" eyes) the seamier side of life. More interesting is the recasting of Trimalchio as Woodcock, a vulgar but wealthy representative of the lower class who gives an ostentatious banquet and who aspires to be considered a person of culture. The difference of degree, however, is crucial. Petronius' work maintains a cynical attitude toward Trimalchio, whereas Wells's novel suggests that Woodcock may embody the hope of humanity's future. Woodcock, who "out of a dream . . . had got [a] crazy confidence" (AP, 325), finally departs from Parham, with whom he has shared a similar yet slightly different sense of purpose and destiny. Parham is left in the dream world of the *Satyricon*, whereas Woodcock, as a revised version of Trimalchio, enters another, somewhat more optimistic version of this same "reality."

In effect such a revision of Petronius' Classical text constitutes a management of reader expectations. If he realizes the parallel between the *Satyricon* and *Parham*, the reader must confront whatever disappointments of these expectations may arise; so in *Parham*, as in other early and late novels by Wells, the emphasis of Wells's technique falls on the cognitive processes of the reader. This novel, in other words, points away from itself as a self-contained, finished artifact—the way history appears to Parham—and towards the reader's cognitive experience of open-ended possibility in the novel and in his own life. More directly than Petronius' cynical satire, Wells's novel lampoons its characters in the hope of revising human behavior. Ideally, for Wells, *Parham* should function as a self-consuming artifact, a work with a distinctive identity, derived from its modification of the *Satyricon* model, that finally does not exist for itself (i.e., as an example of art-for-art's-sake) and yields its individuality in the process of exposing readers to multiple realities in time. Like the text of *Parham* as a revised echo of the *Satyricon*, like all historical events and personality types, every reader, in Wells's view, paradoxically blends uniqueness (individuality) and typicality.

The ideal reader of *Parham* should awaken from his present dream-reality, as does Woodcock in the dream-novel in the hands of the reader. Herein lies an explanation for the following intrusive comment occurring in the last chapter: "A dream, as everyone knows, can happen with incredible rapidity. It may all have happened in a second" (AP, 321). Any event in history, it follows, indeed all of history as the reader has experienced it, is like a second in some larger unobserved time scheme incorporating simultaneous alternate possibilities. The reader's entire life, the novel indicates, amounts to such a second or, more accurately, to such a dream-second:

> All life has something dreamlike in it. No percipient creature has ever yet lived in stark reality. Nature has equipped us with such conceptions and delusions as survival necessitated, and our experiences are at best but working interpretations. Nevertheless, as they diverge more and more from practical truth and we begin to stumble against danger, our dearest dreams are at last invaded by remonstrances and warning shadows. (AP, 250)

The "truth" hinted at in *Parham* is designed by Wells to puncture the dream of the reader's firm sense of history and of personality, or self. Just as Parham and Woodcock awaken from their similar dreams, the reader ought to awaken from the dream of the text he is reading; and in the process of managing whatever disappointments or surprises generated by the revision of the *Satyricon* model as well as coping with the deprivation of fictive illusion whenever the narrative voice bursts through the essentially conventional manner of the novel, the reader should awaken out of the present phase of his dream-life to participate, with Woodcock, in another one—one similar yet different in degree insofar as it involves a more advanced condition of human self-awareness. Wells denies his reader any escape into the past time of history, the present time of contemporary personality, or the future time of the speculative events of his humorous novel; his object remains to decrease self-delusion by rousing the reader from all such related forms of fictive time in texts and in life.

In achieving this end in *Parham* Wells manages the technique of the splintering frame. In other words, indicating the negative as well as the positive feaures of the human dream-reality—by positing an equation of the dreams of its characters, the "dream" of the reader vicariously experiencing the illusory text, and the dream of each reader's personal experience of history and personality in life—*Parham* becomes a self-consuming artifact, a work which surrenders any fixed identity based on its Classical prototype or as a permanent work of art and which generates an actual response in its readers.

In contrast to Parham's concept of art as "the concentrated quality of loveliness" resulting from selectivity and permanence (AP, 20, 23), the novel in which he exists ironically exhibits a fragmentation and a fluidity similar to the incomplete and progressive jazz music which irritates him (AP, 48). This deliberate manner frustrates any hope in the reader for discernible structural firmness in the novel and, consequently, for his comfortable engagement with the fictive illusion of the text's humor. Early in the novel minor narrative intrusions occasionally vex the reader's desire to escape into this humor (e.g., AP, 55, 58); however, a major violation of the reader's relaxed submergence into the dream-story occurs when the narrative voice suddenly dismisses all of Book One and the first chapter of Book Two of the novel as "a certain prelude," if not quite a false start:

> But the real business we have in hand in this book is to tell of the Master Spirit. A certain prelude has been necessary to our story, but now that we are through with it we can admit it was no more than a prelude. Here at the earliest possible moment the actual story starts. There shall be nothing else but story-telling now right to the end of the book. (AP, 90)

At this juncture the reader's sense of dislocation is quite significant, as the satirical phase of the novel most reminiscent of the *Satyricon* becomes increasingly modified. Confronting this fragmentation of the novel, this apparently structure-defying division recalling Parham's fear of the crumbling of definite lines, the reader senses his victimization by a confidence-man narrator who has lured the reader thus far into the story for some purpose other than mere humorous entertainment. And, it follows, what should the reader make of the narrator's explicit promise to tell only a story henceforth, after his violation of the same implicit promise a reader assumes every novelist to make? Surely the reader ought to remain skeptical after this experience of dislocation — and with good reason. First, the second half, or fragment, of the novel includes a disturbing revision of reader sympathy for the refined Parham in the first half; increasingly, in contrast to Petronius' treatment of Trimalchio, Woodcock emerges (in spite of initial reader hostility towards his vulgarity) as the genuine protagonist of the book. Second, most of the novel is merely a dream, as the reader discovers only at the end of the book, a dream from which the characters awaken and into the narrative frame of which the narrator intrudes (as we saw) to comment on the dreamlike nature of life.

After this critical transition to the second part of the novel, the reader is never permitted easy reliance upon fictional convention or sure identification of narrator or authorial loyalty towards the characters. Never resolved, this uncertainty informs the final words of the novel:

> And so, showing a weary back to us, with his evening hat on the back of his head, our deflated publicist [Parham] recedes up Pontingale Street, recedes with all his vanities, his stores of erudition, his dear preposterous generalizations, his personified nations and all his obsolescent paraphernalia of scholarly political wisdom, so feebly foolish in their substance and so hideously disastrous in their possible consequences, and his author, who has come to feel a curious unreasonable affection for him, must needs bid him a reluctant farewell. (AP, 328)

Of course, in the last analysis, good sense can be made of this apparent authorial vacillation concerning Parham; in fact this very search for understanding, this requisite cognition by the reader defines the purpose of these closing words. The quaint Victorian mannerism of these final words, so vexed by the paradoxically satirical/sympathetic attitude of the narrator, fractures the fictional convention it pretends to employ, thereby once more splintering the frame of the novel and generating for a last time an experience of dislocation in the reader. In a sense, the reader briefly loses his place, even at the book's close where presumably the reader ought to feel most confident. The reader's experience here is different only in degree from that of Parham, who in confronting the seeming threat of "definite lines crumbled" is authorially described as "a

63

reader who has lost his place in a story and omitted to turn down the page" (AP, 192)—a remark designed by Wells to be reflexive in its implicit analogy between Parham and the Parham-like reader, and the life-dream and the text-dream. In *Parham* the frame of the text splinters, even at the end, so that its dream-fiction points away from artistic self-enclosure and thrusts outwardly through its fictional perimeter into the realm of the reader.

Commencing as a modern-day *Satyricon*, Wells's novel revises its Classical prototype, with which it is similar in discursive and fragmentary manner but from the satire of which it differs somewhat concerning the nature of humanity. This revision is aesthetically conveyed through the technique of "the splintering frame," which procedure violates reader expectations based on fictional conventions. In this way denying escape through humor in *Parham*, Wells shatters his reader's Parham-like illusions about historical events, personality types, and human prospects—about the dream of life in general. The true Master Spirit in *Parham*, anticipating the significance of the possible Martian incursion in *Star Begotten*, is the self-awareness which Wells hopes will invade the dream-reality of each reader, who ideally should awaken to discover that he is living his life in the same sort of vicarious escapism characteristic of the average reader's experience of a typical humorous work. This "invaded" and roused reader should for a moment have a sense of losing his place in the dream-fiction of his present life, so that he may henceforth participate better in the true story of humanity, "the actual story" of the Master Spirit. Not characterized by delusively rigid structures, this story, like *Parham*, expresses a dreamlike fluidity of self and event that permits open-ended possibilities for an evolutionary transformation of human existence little imagined at present.

Exhausting the *Bildungsroman*

Vexation of the reader's complacency, as exemplified in *The Autocracy of Mr. Parham*, surfaces time and again in several subsequent works Wells wrote in a genre of the novel he found particularly attractive, the *Bildungsroman*. With the appearance of Thomas Carlyle's translation of Goethe's *Wilhelm Meister* (1827), the *Bildungsroman* steadily worked its way into the English literary imagination, so much so that many significant Victorian novels belong to this tradition. These works range from Brontë's *Jane Eyre* (1847), to Thackeray's *Pendennis* (1848-50) and Dickens' *Great Expectations* (1860-61), and later from Hardy's *Jude the*

Obscure (1895) to Lawrence's *The Rainbow* (1915) and Joyce's *Portrait of the Artist as a Young Man* (1916). Generally the *Bildungsroman*, which includes the *Künstlerroman* (concerning the artist), depicts the development of a young person, a sensitive protagonist undergoing various initiatory experiences which contribute to that protagonist's maturation and acquisition of sufficient understanding of life to find a place in it for him- or herself. Often the protagonist is orphaned, a condition of vulnerability that eventually leads to the independent formation of a character and of a standard of values in accord with the ideals of Victorian community. This formula for the protagonist's success in the *Bildungsroman* did not remain unmutated during the Victorian period, as Meredith's *Ordeal of Richard Feveral* (1859) and Eliot's *Mill on the Floss* (1860) demonstrate; and substantial agitation, even inversion of the formulae of the genre occurred in late- and post-Victorian fiction, particularly, say, in Hardy's *Jude the Obscure* and Lawrence's *The Rainbow*.[3] Just as in both of these later novels climaxes do not coincide with reader expectations engendered by the formulae of the *Bildungsroman*, similar conventions undergo revision in Wells's experiments in the genre from *Tono-Bungay* onward.[4]

During the Thirties Wells's fascination with the *Bildungsroman* produced *The Bulpington of Blup* (1932), *The Anatomy of Frustration* (1937), *The Brothers* (1938) and *The Holy Terror* (1939). In most of these works Wells tends to devote his creative energy chiefly to inversions of generic patterns, particularly in the matter of authorial sympathy for the protagonist. However, the impression given by these works suggests that Wells found the discursiveness of the *Bildungsroman* a mite too comfortable. Although in three of these works Wells's art fails to attain the level of excellence manifested by other works he wrote during the Thirties, each possesses some merit. The urgent brevity of *The Brothers*, for example, is balanced by the novel's "antitypical" revision of Anthony Hope's *The Prisoner of Zenda* (1894),[5] and the plodding discursiveness of *The Holy Terror* is balanced by the work's "antitypical" advancement of Suetonius' *The Twelve Caesars*. In terms of this amalgamation of the "typical" *Bildungsroman* and the typology of other kinds of writing, *The Anatomy* emerges as a major artistic innovation. In this work Wells combined the *Bildungsroman* and the bio-critical study. Moreover, he advanced the *Bildungsroman* by replacing the usual youthful socially-oriented protagonist with a young sensitive mind undergoing experiences with various ideas. The plot of the traditional *Bildungsroman* is replaced in *The Anatomy* by a series of speculations on various subjects, a series given a somewhat arbitrary and inadequate arrangement by an editor. This mutation of the *Bildungsroman* emphasizes an internal (mental), rather than an external (social) development representative of the collective human mind. In its artistic management of these two revisions *The Anatomy* far surpasses Wells's three other efforts during the Thirties to effect an evolved version of the *Bildungsroman* which would now admit a fourth dimension, a greater timeliness or relevance to the reader.

Emending the *Bildungsroman* in *The Anatomy* involves for Wells a number of other revisions, including an adaptation of the prototypical text of Robert Burton's *The Anatomy of Melancholy* (1621), of Nietzsche's concept of the superman, and of Schopenhauer's ideas about will and frustration (AF, 2, 12, 36). Significantly, too, *The Anatomy of Frustration* reviews and modifies Wells's earlier beliefs. In *The Anatomy*, as Robert Philmus has remarked, Wells "virtually recreates himself as his own 'precursor.' That is, he suggests new ways of looking at, and supplies new terms for speaking about, the concepts operative in his fiction—and with them a new perspective in his development as a writer." Assessing the essential ambivalence in Wells's writings, early and late, and correlating it to the division between descriptive analysis and prescriptive synthesis in the book, Philmus concludes:

> *The Anatomy* thus brings together Wells's diverse concerns as a writer. It does so not simply through its content, through the ambivalent balance between analysis and syntheses, but also in its form. By combining the fictional elements of a life of Steele with the descriptive elements of an exposition of his thought, it points to a continuity between Wells's novels and his nonfictional prose.[6]

This cogent reading can be deepened when Wells's personal revisionism, as expressed through the integration of tract and fiction, is scrutinized as a recasting of the *Bildungsroman*, particularly of its structural framework.

The word *framework* abounds in *The Anatomy*. Referring most often to ideological frameworks, this recurrent image suggests Wells's primary interest in structure in the work. As the following discussion indicates, the technique of the splintering frame in *The Anatomy* represents the possibility of a mental ideological framework more encompassing than the one provided by the text in hand, though it in fact emerges from within the very narrative of that text.

Central to Wells's management of structure in *The Anatomy* is *enchâssement*, setting narratives within narratives. In the text proper the outer frame is provided by the voice of the narrator, who is writing a synthetic bio-critical study of William Burroughs Steele. This frame constitutes a revision of Paul Jordan-Smith's *Bibliographia Burtoniana: A Study of Robert Burton's The Anatomy of Melancholy* (1931), which the narrator mentions (AF, 4). Within this narrative frame is the voice of Steele, the author of the multivolume *Anatomy of Frustration* designed to synthesize beyond and so emend Burton's exemple in *The Anatomy of Melancholy*. Steele, according to the critic-narrator, at first imitated Burton, who in Steele's opinion despaired concerning the irrational universe and so adopted "the mask of 'Democritus Junior' " when conveying his impression of human helplessness (AF, 7). Afterwards, the narrator observes, Steele ceased to imitate Burton and discovered that his own work ought "to be not so much a modernization of Burton as a counterpart" (AF, 4), especially in the matter of affirming the possibility of an optimistic response to a problematic universe. By means of *enchâssement* Wells not only maintains a dialectical engagement of pessimism and optimism, he also suggests an evolution of syntheses from Burton's assembly of quotations "giving every aspect of opinion its turn," through Steele's revision and somewhat more clarified "huge work remain[ing] clumsy and unfinished," to the critic-narrator's incomplete endeavor to rearrange Steele's work (AF, 7, 201).

The narrator's effort is far from conclusive, a fact exemplified for instance in no less than four attempts in Chapter Nineteen to organize Steele's ideas about frustration and loneliness. The narrator's work cannot be completed because (in accordance with the notion of time as a spiral that now informs Wells's typology of texts and characterization) human mental evolution is infinitely expansive, every human statement "a trial framework" (AF, 128) to be revised in turn. Just as the work of each of the three authors in *The Anatomy* is "not an exact repetition" but "a parallel at another level," so throughout human time generally "the good things will be said again and again and said better" (AF, 46, 203). "Being is rhythm," the narrator reports, reflecting on Steele's speculation that "perhaps there is no straight line of behaviour for any living thing, perhaps it is better to come back continually to your essential point than to try to stay there" (AF, 145). Located in a parallel but different level of the expanding spiral of human consciousness, which evolves in time with increasing speed, Burton comprehended more than his predecessor Democritus, Steele more than Burton, the narrator more than Steele, and (the text therapeutically intimates) the reader more than the narrator.

This final emphasis on the reader results from an evolution of focus in *The Anatomy*. Initially the book permits Burton to figure in the reader's consciousness, but quickly Burton is superseded in importance by Steele. As the narrative advances, even Steele's centrality is gradually displaced by the steady emergence of the narrator as the protagonist of his critical study of Steele. At first the narrator appears as a mere editor briefly recounting, after the example of Jordan-Smith on Burton, a few details about Steele's life and then in his redactions subserviently following the order of ideas presented by Steele. Yet, when he remarks, "He never brought together all his notes upon this idea; they remain mostly un-printed among his residual papers, and I mention them here, because here seems the right place" (AF, 37-38), the narrator is not merely busy devoting himself to a redaction but of necessity is struggling to integrate various, somewhat unmanageable manuscripts. And when he says, in this particular instance, that these notes ought to be dismissed, he anticipates later intrusions into his narrative, intrusions expressing explicit disagreement with Steele (e.g., AF, 79, 98). This development touches the issue of the dialectical revisionism at the heart of *The Anatomy* and also subtly contributes to the movement of the narrator to the foreground of his account. Indeed, the text before the reader represents the narrator's synthesis and it occasionally exhibits his pride, his ego, in having im-proved upon the work of his subject: "This, I think is a novel and useful way of attacking the problems" (AF, 112). Sometimes the narrator un-wittingly reveals a degree of antagonism toward his subject or, perhaps, a lack of sympathy: "It is amusing to read Steele as he tries to be broad-minded and patient and confident in the necessity of progress, while all the time he is fretting against his facts" (AF, 124). Increasingly the narrator modifies his "framing" role as restrained critic of and collabora-tor in "Steele's ideas" (AF, 74), until very late in the work he even boldly "introduce[s] a critical section under a heading that Steele never employed" (AF, 197). By the end of his book the narrator's voice not only has functioned as the outer frame but also paradoxically has emerged as the vital center of the account:

There are times when I turn over these bales and folders of Steele's, which, in their queer way, in their quaint simulation of an encyclopaedic index and summary, do evoke a vision of all human literature and history and experience, and it seems to me that his aspirations are no more than the voice of a lost creature crying in the night. And then again I find it is not so. I realize with a start that I am beginning to see things about me more clearly than I used to do before I set myself to explore the world with him. What were once dark impenetrable masses are taking on form and detail. And then it is that same valiant note among his memoranda rings out like a cock crow and I find that I, too, am moved to believe that this dawn of a greater life, this New Beginning, this world revlution, does now impend. (AF, 214)

Who is this narrator? Precisely *who* does not matter, for he is a more evolved type in the Burton-Steele mold. What matters is his dual position as frame and center of his tract-novel, which position represents (in Wells's opinion) the true place of the collective human type. This human type manifests—Wells here revises Schopenhauer's notion of Will—a force, a divinelike collective will (AF, 49, 216) comprised of freedom and fate in dialectic. Fate finds expression in the framework of ideas; freedom finds expression in a thrust against this framework, and it arises from *within* the "framework of the ["multidimensional"] mind" (AF, 184, 189, 202). This exertion of the collective will splinters the framework from within and it does this *ad infinitum* through an evolutionary process (AF, 129) which expands the fate expressed in personal individuality or ego, which in turn is supported by a framework of ideas. Behind the "fate" of a framework of ideas at any given moment of time is—and here Wells revises a Nietzschean concept—an immanent "super individuality (not a super individual N. B.) arising out of the species" that "is the sum of human knowledge and expression, the sustaining consciousness, the reasonable will of the race" (AF, 36). The narrator manifests this *typical* "super individuality" more than does Steele, who manifests it more than does Burton, who manifests it more than does Democritus. So Steele's voice expands and re-creates Burton's framework of ideas, and the critic-narrator's voice expands and re-creates Steele's framework of ideas.

Implied here too is the reader's responsibility to contribute his voice. Ideally the reader should participate in this process of expansion through the Logos-power engendered by the collective will within the human self. As the outermost frame in the dynamics of reading (reader and text), the reader is left with unresolved matters, such as the narrator's four starts in Chapter Nineteen, the unanswered question of whether Burton and Steele committed suicide, and the uncertainty over whether the text in hand is tract, fiction, or bio-critical study. This manner, reflecting Wells's technique of the splintering frame, engages the reader in cognition, in an internal expansion through thought necessitating "criticism of and collaboration in" the process of expanding ideological frames in the text and in life. Through the revisionism implicit in the act of sorting out, the reader's thoughts become in effect the new and (for the present) outermost frame of *The Anatomy.*

This structural pattern of expansion from within comprises the fourth dimensional aesthetic of *The Anatomy*, a "timely" work suggesting the limitless multidimensional framework of the informed/in-forming human mind. *The Anatomy* is timely in engaging the relativity of the reader at a specific moment in time and also in eschewing any firm narrative architectonic pattern for its ideas. Positing only a permanent revisionism, *The Anatomy* represents merely one timely act in this on-going process of expanding reader relativity. "There are no immortal works of art"; art participates in an evolution, through time, of a typology of texts, just as each artist (in accord with Romantic tradition) advances the artist Type: "In art predestination is everything. . . . The business of the artist in any field is the enlargement of appreciation. He is a mutation. He is the growing point of the species. He is perpetually expanding the field for the play of the human imagination" (AF, 202, 204). As exemplified by the use of the medium of a bio-critical study to present fiction, artistic freedom in *The Anatomy* enlarges the predestined form of the *Bildungsroman*, just as each level of voice in the work revises and amplifies the preceding voice it "contains" within itself and just as the tentative prescriptive synthesis of the work emends and augments the descriptive analysis of Wells's earlier writings that lies "within" this synthesis. This freedom, interacting dialectically with the fate of form, splinters the framework and so "expand[s] the field for the play of the human imagination" by evoking the evolving cognition of the reader, whose thoughts comprise the new outermost frame of the work.

Structured in terms of parallel, yet evolved, framing voices, including the reader's thoughts self-consciously generated in the mind, *The Anatomy* revises the *Bildungsroman*. It depicts the steady emergence or development of the quintessential human type (AF, 35; cf. KW, 27) underlying all personalities throughout time, specifically the individuality of Democritus, Burton, Steele, the narrator, and the reader. *The Anatomy* exhibits a self-awareness resulting in a dialectical encounter between the predestined conventional form of the *Bildungsroman*, or fiction in general, and the impulse of artistic freedom to mutate predetermined forms. This internal dialectic concerning the form of the *Bildungsroman* in *The Anatomy* parallels the tension between fate and freedom and the opposition between Wells's past views and his present attitudes. This same internal dialectic informs the ongoing revision of each successive frame of cognition provided by Democritus, Burton, Steele, the narrator, and the reader. All these concerns, aesthetically embodied in the structural technique of the splintering frame, disclose for Wells how the *Bildungsroman*, like all art, is as multidimensional in its evolutionary possibilities as is the multidimensional framework of the human mind from which it originates. Its *in-forming* structure derives from the human mind for the purpose of *informing* that same mind; as a result this mind ideally ought to evolve farther along the, as it were, spiral pattern engendered by this in-forming/informing. By conveying this meta-statement about itself as an art work in process, *The Anatomy* at once exhausts and amplifies the *Bildungsroman*.

Exorcising the Ghost Story

Similar to his life-long artistic interest in dreams, so maturely managed in *The Autocracy of Mr. Parham*, Wells's fascination with the ghost story surfaced during the earliest phase of his literary career. Then, in fact, Edwardian culture indulged in the genre, perhaps as an unconscious expression of its *fin-de-siècle* fear of insubstantiality. From the first, however, Wells characteristically criticised the practitioners and the conventions of the genre. This is evident in his well-crafted "The Inexperienced Ghost" (in *Twelve Stories and a Dream*, 1903) and his review of Sheridan LeFanu's *The Evil Guest* (1895). LeFanu, Wells complained, mastered little more than the method of "piling it on," which manner ultimately dissipated any sense of horror. Moreover, Wells observed, LeFanu, among others, failed to work within the tradition established by Edgar Allan Poe, that "consummate creator of strange effects."[7] Poe figured importantly in Wells's artistic self-awareness during these early years, and Wells readily compared books by Edmund S. Gunn, George MacDonald and several other Scotch novelists to Poe's works.[8] In turn, the earliest reviewers of Wells's romances and short tales consistently referred to similarities to Poe's manner, though in fact to date little of substance has been remarked concerning Poe's influence on Wells. Nor have critics noticed the extent to which interest in Poe was expressed even in the latest phases of Wells's career. In the early Thirties Wells alluded to Poe (EA, 71, 78), as he did in the late Twenties in proposed advertisement copy he personally prepared for *Mr. Blettsworthy on Rampole Island*: "of the fantastic events . . . we can give no conception here. As soon might we summarize a romance by Edgar Allan Poe."[9]

In fact Poe wrote few works which could properly be designated as ghost stories. Doubtless Wells, who also wrote very few ghost stories, admired Poe most for his precise "bearing of structural expedients upon design" and for his mastery of "the necessary trick of commonplace detail which renders horrors convincing."[10] Anticipating his prefatory comments in *Scientific Romances* (1933),[11] pertaining to the best method for writing science fiction, Wells's observation about commonplace detail and convincing horror describes perfectly the stylistic technique of *The Croquet Player* (1936), in which the narrator confesses to a boyhood addiction to Poe's writings (CP, 38).

The Croquet Player is a first person plotless narrative recounting the unnerving experiences and conversations of an upper class young man, who by the end of his account casually dismisses the urgency of the apparently apocalyptic implications of the emergence of various types of malevolence in Cainsmarsh. Georgie Frobisher, the idle narrator of *The Croquet Player*, refers to his tale as "a sort of ghost story," one "much more realistic and haunting and disturbing than any ordinary ghost story" (CP, 1-2). Initially his account appears to conform to a fundamental pattern of the genre: the characters are victims who do not *seem* to deserve the problem which emerges and who experience displacement of their sense of life as rationally ordered by exposure to an agnostic world where explanations are impossible and values are unstable.[12] But Frobisher's authorially-directed qualification "sort of" is critical, for in his narrative the sensationalism for its own sake typical of late Victorian and turn-of-the-century ghost stories like LeFanu's gives way to moral purposes well beyond those evident in the occult novels of, say, Margaret Oliphant and Edward Bulwer-Lytton.[13]

Reminiscent of the depiction of human existence in Poe's works, life as presented in *The Croquet Player* includes a latent subterranean force threatening serene commonplace activity. "Below the surface" of average daily behavior, Frobisher observes retrospectively, lurks "an unhappy, wicked spirit," something "bestial" which theological thought attributes to the legacy of Cain or to the influence of devils and which post-Darwinian scientific thought designates as a repressed caveman disposition for "cruelty, suspicion and ape-like malice" (CP, 29, 34, 35, 40). In the modern world of the Thirties, however, this powerful, irrational force can no longer be repressed, a fact made manifest by the archaeological unearthing of the human past and by the psychological delving into the underground of the human mind. That both of these parallel activities reveal a disconcerting reality underlying humanity and its civilization is implied in Dr. Finchatton's nightmare, which also specifically depicts the rise of militarism in the mid-Thirties:

More and more did the threat of that primordial Adamite dominate me. I could not banish that eyeless stare and that triumphant grin [of a Paleolithic skull] from my mind, sleeping or waking. Waking I saw it as it was in the museum, as if it was a living presence that had set us a riddle and was amused to hear our inadequate attempts at a solution. Sleeping I saw it released from all rational proportions. It became gigantic. It became as vast as a cliff, a mountainous skull in which the orbits and hollows of the jaw were huge caves. He had an effect — it is hard to convey these dream effects — as if he was continually rising and yet he was always towering there. In the foreground I saw his innumerable descendants, swarming like ants, swarms of human beings hurrying to and fro, making helpless gestures of submission or deference, resisting an over-powering impulse to throw themselves under his all devouring shadow. Presently these swarms began to fall into lines and columns, were clad in uniforms, formed up and began marching and trotting towards the black shadows under those worn and rust-stained teeth. From which darkness there presently oozed something — something winding and trickling, and something that manifestly tasted very agreeably to him. Blood. (CP, 55-56)

By coalescing archaeological find and psychological disclosure Wells here provides an emblem for the human condition, a modern emblem equivalent in effect, say, to Poe's use of the skull as an underlying design in "The Gold Bug" and "The Fall of the House of Usher."

Unlike the typical ghost story, however, *The Croquet Player* does not completely obscure the issue of cause and effect, with the result that in a special sense possibilities are not blocked for its characters. The ancestral skull, now visible within the underground of human civilization "like something being lit up behind a transparency," provides "an explanation that [is] itself an enigma" (CP, 64); and however engimatic its explanation, it intimates a cause-and-effect verity encouraging rather than denying the assertion of human will. Dr. Norbert, an agitated and prophetic psychotherapist, makes this point when he speaks of a possible supra-rational cure for the "new Plague" evident "all over the world" in *"intellectual men . . . going mad"* because the "cave-man who is over us, who is in us, and who is indeed *us,* is going against [our] imaginary selves" (CP, 69, 75). "There will be no choice before a human being," Norbert continues, "but to be either a driven animal or a stern devotee to that civilization, that disciplined civilization, that has never yet been achieved," "such a mental effort as the stars have never witnessed yet. Arise, O mind of Man!" (CP, 76, 78). This emphasis on cause and effect, on possibility of resolution, and on primacy of human rationality and will is uncharacteristic of the conventional ghost story, including Poe's tales of horror.

In the traditional ghost story plot is weak, authorial stress given to a style designed to induce a particular sensation in the reader. Although the style of *The Croquet Player* is effectively managed, neither it nor the plot engage Wells as much as does the "bearing of structural expedients upon design." The structure of *The Croquet Player* recalls the Poesque devices Wells used in *The Time Machine*, especially the creation of a narrator who directly addresses/represents the reader and who relates the words and actions of another (who may signify, as in psychomachia, a mental part of the narrator/reader). When the narrator thinks he is "like that wedding guest who was gripped by the Ancient Mariner" and refers to his account as "apocalyptic" (CP, 75, 82), the author behind him hints at a revision of *The Time Machine*, to which both remarks are germane. Whereas pessimism pervades this earlier romance, the fear of a possible "new Plague" of atavism resulting from the principle of regression (as defined in Darwin's *The Descent of Man*, 1871) is balanced in *The Croquet Player* by a therapeutic hope in prescriptive evolutionary synthesis. Aesthetically this therapy finds principal embodiment in Wells's revision of the structuring narrative frame of the earlier work.

Speaking of himself as a "frame" (CP, 8), Frobisher narrates an account which encloses or frames Dr. Finchatton's story. This Chinese-box technique of enclosing a story within a story includes intimations of a parallelism between the account as rendered to the reader and the framed narrative as rendered to the narrator. Frobisher and Finchatton share more than somewhat similar names; they give identical reasons for recounting their stories. Frobisher's explanation that he writes primarily in a therapeutic attempt to clear up matters and gain reassurance from his readers echoes Finchatton's need to speak in order to hear how the narrative sounds (CP, 1, 12). This pattern likewise emerges in the report given to Finchatton by the achaeologist at Eastfolk Museum—a story enclosed within the narrative that is itself enclosed within the frame—"as if he was trying out his ideas" (CP, 47). Again, just as Frobisher commences with "a few particulars about" himself, Finchatton begins with "a touch of autobiography" (CP, 2, 14). Such an elaborate framing apparatus in fiction sometimes hints at something ominous, even while it initially invites reader comfort;[14] in *The Croquet Player* it functions in this manner in a muted way. Deftly managed, the framing technique of this novel initially seems to invite the reader to experience enclosure as insulation and security. In final effect, however, the framing device intimates the real menacing presence of an underground life in the human self, something covered over by, as it were, layers of egotism—self-enclosing layers similar to strata hiding humanity's primitive ancestry, skin concealing humanity's ape-like skull, and narrative frames encircling some obscure hidden truth.

This tendency of Frobisher and, by implication, of his readers to seek patterns of insularity (as an effect of egotism on the self) is, for Wells, a Victorian inheritance. Significantly, in his efforts to escape haunted Cainsmarsh, which (as Finchatton's nightmare of the skull suggests) is at once a physical and a mental landscape, Frobisher refuses to "open a book later than Dickens" (CP, 17). Escape into fiction or art generally and the application of antiquated Victorian fictive models (the past) to modern life specifically come under attack in *The Croquet Player*, which Wells designed to reflect the rupture of old social attitudes during the Thirties. Indicting civilization as an "artistic, fictitious," pseudo-orderly "world of Gods and Providences, rainbow promises and so forth," Dr. Norbert hints that the popular novels people favor reinforce their delusions about progress (CP, 73). These delusions about progress and about a framing Providence or rainbow comprise as it were, a comforting and insulating layering characteristic of the human self's egotistical self-enclosure; and it is artistically manifested, in Wells's opinion, in the patterns of Victorian fiction reinforcing that self and its civilization. Beneath or within this layering "nothing [is] secured" (CP, 73); in reality life inside and outside the self is as repetitive as it is progressive—a notion correlating the image of the ape in *The Croquet Player* to Wells's typology of characterization and of texts generally. This life yields an enigmatic explanation or an inexplicable pattern which includes irrationality in the self and asymmetry in the world.

For Wells, the patterns of conventional ghost stories conform to the illusion engendered by Victorian fiction generally. In the traditional ghost story framing, or narrative layering, usually tends toward an enclosure permitting the reader a wide margin of safe distance from the horror. In particular, the reader of the traditional ghost story often senses that the supernatural has no ready referents in the material world outside the fictional frame, an effect created in part by distancing the reader from the central event through multiple layers of narrative. In one sense, of course, this manner can make the central event more dramatic and it might impart an impression of some ineffable enigma (as it does in certain works by James and Conrad). In the typical Victorian ghost story, however, such effects are balanced by a more benign development,

75

through *enchâssement,* of a protective distance between reader and event. Aware of the latter feature and critical of its reflection of how people delusively insulate themselves from reality, Wells revised the device of the framed narrative in *The Croquet Player* so that it could serve the structural purpose of eliciting and then violating the reader's comfortable, conventional expectations associated with the formulaic ghost story. Just as in the novel archaeologists are said to dig beneath layers of dirt to unearth humanity's buried past and just as in the novel psychotherapists are said to penetrate layers of egotism to reveal humanity's bestial self, Wells's "archaeological" and "therapeutic" artistry requires the breaking of the strata of Frobisher's narrative. The multiple story-within-a-story pattern of *The Croquet Player* does not finally yield an apocalyptic revelation at the center of its layered text; it avoids the decisive moment of the direct appearance of the horror, so characteristic of Poe's works. Rather, Wells's novel splinters its frame or opens outwardly, as does the new truth (so disturbing to Frobisher's acquaintances) revealed by modern archaeologists and psychotherapists; as Finchatton remarks concerning the "breaking [of] the frame of our present" in 1936: "We lived in a magic sphere and we felt taken care of and safe. And now in the last century or so, we have broken that. We have poked into the past, unearthing age after age and we peer more and more forward into the future. And that's what's the matter with us"; "the frame of the present was shattered and could never be restored. I had to open out ... and enlarge my mind to a vaster world where the cave-man was as present as the daily [news]paper and a thousand years ahead was on the doorstep" (CP, 48-49, 50-51). Similarly, *The Croquet Player* opens outwardly, does not enclose the horror but releases it upon the reader.

Consider the conclusion of Frobisher's narrative. Quite conventionally the ending of his story returns the reader to its opening, formally suggesting a sense of closure. Indeed, the reader is particularly reminded of the narrator's desire to gain perspective (CP, 1, 79). Yet a crucial distortion occurs in the final words of the book:

> [Dr. Norbert] made a move almost as though he would impede my retreat. He just wanted to go on being apocalyptic. But I had had enough of this apocalyptic stuff.
> I looked him in the face, firmly but politely. I said, "I don't care. The world *may* be going to pieces. The Stone Age may be returning. This may, as you say, be the sunset of civilization. I am sorry, but I can't help it this morning. I have other engagements. All the same—laws of the

Medes and Persians—I am going to play croquet with my aunt at half-past twelve today." (CP, 81-82)

In contrast to countless narrators of conventional ghost stories, Frobisher concludes with disinterest, and in doing so he becomes, or should become, the horror for the reader. The narrator's final attitude of disinterest, implying his desire to insulate himself from reality by living only on the surface of life—he said he was the frame of his narrative—lingers beyond the end of the text to haunt the reader. The horror, then, is not where or what the reader of conventional ghost stories of the period would expect; the horror is the ghost of unreason and ineffective will in the narrator, in the very frame rather than at the center of the story. The horror lurks in the spirit of English civilization (suggested by the narrator's name George and by his fondness for croquet)—in short, in the typical English reader, who as the obvious audience of *The Croquet Player* comprises the outermost frame in the dynamics of reader and text.

The shattered frame of Wells's "journalistic" artistry opens out into the future, just as Finchatton's vision of the future is forecast in the newspaper on his doorstep. This future lies within the "haunted" reader, who perhaps may yet be aroused to assert will and participate in the collective "mind of Man." Herein lies the revision of the pessimism concerning "the sunset of civilization" reflected in *The Time Machine*. Still, in effect the optimism here remains very tentative, a mere question: how will you, the reader, respond to the horror buried within you, the horror of an ineffective will? This irresolved conclusion, this implied question comprises a final instance of the fragmentation of narrative frame in *The Croquet Player*.

Splintering the frame, through management of narrative voice for the purpose of provoking cognition in the reader, occurs as well in *The Camford Visitation* (1937), another of Wells's late attempts to exorcise the ghost story of sensationalism for its own sake. Quite possibly this novel may have been a belated response to W. Earl Hodgson's *Haunted by Posterity* (1895), a story about a man haunted by ghosts from the future that Wells in an early review criticised for exhibiting "one really magnificent idea gone to waste."[15] More certain in this story is Wells's conscious revision of his earliest writings, specifically *The Invisible Man* (1898). In *The Camford Visitation* scientific objections to the sort of invisible man presented in Wells's turn-of-the-century romance are explicitly endorsed (CV, 13-14) so that in the later novel a revised version can emerge as the Voice, an invisible visitor from a "dimension" within the

77

human mind (CV, 25-27) who lectures the academic community of Camford and Oxbridge (i.e., Cambridge and Oxford) about humanity's shortcomings.

The narrative voice of the novel belongs to an unidentified journalist who gives an impression of objectivity as he sifts through various accounts of the reactions of dons and students to an invisible visitor who lectures them on humanity's shortcomings. Occasionally he provides data corroborating reports of encounters with the Voice; most of the time he expresses a "proper" skepticism. The latter is exemplified when he tells the reader,

> It is however a principle hitherto applied chiefly to the evidences for spiritualistic phenomena that any member of imperfectly established cases, any assembly of uncontrolled statements, whatever quality they may have in common do not constitute a scientific proof, and by this standard we are bound to suspend our judgment about all this business. (CV, 52-53)

This appearance of documentary objectivity elicits the reader's confidence in the narrator, whose dispassionately skeptical voice provides the narrative frame of the novel. The reader takes comfort in this frame, trusting it to make sense, which is to say, believing it will contain the story.

This trust, however, becomes vexed at the end of the novel when the narrator reports:

> And as this story goes to press a very interesting brochure comes to hand from the Royal Psychological Society. It is by Dr. Stephen Peter McIntosh. . . . It is a sceptical and destructive examination of the alleged Visitation. He never speaks of it as the Visitation simply, always as the "alleged Visitation." (CV, 72)

McIntosh's work, one might at first assume, to some degree mirrors the manner of the book in the reader's hands. But the narrator's emphasis on "alleged" hints at a distinction, one which in fact becomes clearer when we are told subsequently about the presence of the Voice at a Camford ceremony:

> The reticence of the trained reporters present, he insists, is very significant. In spite of the alleged existence of a complete shorthand report, *The Camford Mail* ignored the incident absolutely, and the words of the speech only became available when the young stenographer who claims to have taken it was dismissed from the staff of that paper. Dr. McIntosh rejects his report as a forgery. (CV, 73-74)

This member of the newspaper staff is never identified in *The Camford*

Visitation, but the alert reader, who remembers that the narrator is a journalist who reports every word spoken by the Voice, might suppose *the possibility* that the narrator is this dismissed staffmember. Such detection, engaging the cognitive processes of the reader, can occur only at the end of the novel, where it suddenly casts a new light on what the reader had initially and innocently accepted as an objective account. The reader now realizes that all the preceding documentation—more accurately, *alleged* documentation—might have been guided by the narrator's covert aim to validate his own report. What the reader at first perceived to be an objective narrative frame shatters, exposing him to the dream-like fiction which comprises his own seemingly real life "framed" by certain similar conventions and expectations. The frame is revealed to be an illusion or dream; "reality is within" (CV, 26), lies at the center of the text, is the Voice.

The Voice, emerging from within the human psyche, passes from the inner narrative, merges with and breaks through the narrative voice framing that Voice, and finally resides within the mind of the reader, the outermost frame in the dynamics of reader and text. The last words of the novel—" 'How can we go on,' cried Trumbler, 'keeping where we are, unless we ignore him?' " (CV, 75)—poses a question reminiscent of all the similar questions asked by the Voice; and it is a question demanding an answer, the use of the reader's *voice*. Presumably if the reader replies properly, he will hear not only his own voice (equivalent to an expanding narrative frame) but the Voice (equivalent to the center of the narrative of human existence) emerging from the human mind and shattering the convention of skepticism typical of the average reader's response. Indeed, in this instance the very traditional structure of question and answer would disappear, for the Voice/voice that asks in actuality is the same voice/Voice that would reply.

The Camford Visitation, then, is no mere story of perverse human desire for invisibility, or transcendence, a desire exemplified by Griffin, for example, in *The Invisible Man*. It modifies the ghost tale to present the invisible Spirit of Man seeking incarnation through the steady expansion of "inner" human reality outwardly into the evolving, ever-more clarified dream of humanity's daily activities. This closure of real "inner" self and "dream" outer self, as expressed in an infinitely shatterable and expanding multidimensional framework of the human mind (as objectified in Wells's experiments with narrative frame), comprises a version of Wells's logology, of his faith in the possibility of the word becoming flesh. By splintering the frame of *The Camford Visitation* and of *The Croquet*

Player so as to make the reader's experience of shattered insularity an extension of that infinitely expandable frame, in fiction as in life, Wells evokes reader relativity, an aesthetic fourth dimension in his art. In this way he revises, enlarges and elevates the ghost story formula, exorcising its typical sensationalism for its own sake by transforming its structural devices into an art form reflecting life (as he assessed it) in the Thirties.

Towards the Ultra-Science-Fiction Novel

Wells's fascination with revising the ghost story formula, the *Bildungsroman*, and such Classical texts as the *Satyricon* and *The Twelve Caesars* always had at its center authorial self-revision. As we have noted previously, Wells engaged in a life-long dialectic resulting in an extensive personal revision. Most pronounced during the Thirties, this personal revision was appropriate to his recognition of an expanding finite universe, of evolutionary theory, and of the relativity of time and art. For Wells, we should recall, a novel is ideally a self-consuming artifact, a work with a distinct identity that finally should not exist for itself but should serve the utilitarian purpose of exposing the reader to multiple human possibilities in time. Within time, that multidimensional framework of the human mind, various unique human species evolve towards an elusive ideal Type as they express a variety of alternate possibilities for humanity, which at any given moment lives as if in a dream. Just as a text and its characters incorporate at once unique and typical identities, so too should their readers sense within themselves the paradoxical blend of individuality and communal type. Wells saw himself as no exception, a fact *Star Begotten: A Biological Fantasia* (1937) makes clear.[16]

A plotless story about the effect on the mind of a popular historian of the various speculations of several people concerning the possible invasion of Earth by Martians using cosmic rays to mutate the human species, *Star Begotten* demonstrates a variety of the splintering frame practiced by Wells. In this instance his structural management is designed to act in dialectic with the framework readers had come to anticipate in a Wellsian science-fiction novel. In the context of this revision Wells apparently viewed the work as an advance towards the ultra-science-fiction novel, an elusive ideal toward which his previous science-fiction novels, by a kind of asymptotic evolution, had been pointing. As we have seen in his adaptation of *Pilgrim's Progress* in *Men Like Gods*, the *Satyricon* in *The Autocracy of Mr. Parham*, *Bibliographia Burtoniana* in *The Anatomy of Frustration*, and the ghost-story formula in *The Croquet Player* and *The Camford Visitation*, among other instances, Wells's typology of texts is founded on his belief that each successive text evinces in time a potential for advancing its type toward perfection. This perfection, however, as Hegel had asserted, this point when form is wholly adequate to content remains unattainable.[17] Appropriately Wells's own early works are included in this revisionary attitude, and in *Star Begotten* references to *The War of the Worlds* (1898) complement allusions to *The Food of the Gods* (1904), *A Modern Utopia* (1905), and *The Outline of History* (1920).

Mention of the first of these works appears early in *Star Begotten* when a minor character remarks:

> Some of you may have read a book called *The War of the Worlds*—I forget who wrote it—Jules Verne, Conan Doyle, one of those fellows. But it told how the Martians invaded the world, wanted to colonize it and exterminate mankind. Hopeless attempt! They couldn't stand the different atmospheric pressure, they couldn't stand the difference in gravitation; bacteria finished them. Hopeless from the start. The only impossible thing in the story was to imagine that the Martians would be fools enough to try anything of the sort. (SB, 50-51)

The work surfaces again later when Joseph Davis, the protagonist of *Star Begotten*, imagines "a Martian as something hunched together, like an octopus, tentacular, saturated with evil poisons, oozing unpleasant juices, a gigantic leathery bladder of hate" (SB, 96). Such allusions invite the reader to anticipate from this science-fiction novel something similar to the invasion formula exhibited in *The War of the Worlds*. *Star Begotten* revises this expectation. Allusions to infection and contagion in the work, applied to humans rather than to Martians and to the mind rather than to the body, indicate a very subtle form of invasion, the possible mutation of humanity by aliens employing cosmic rays; and, as we shall see, the novel violates and revises several other anticipations entertained by the reader.

Revisions of Wells's earlier writings and of the expectations they generate lie behind an unobtrusive allusion to *The Food of the Gods* or to *A Modern Utopia*, or possibly to *Men Like Gods*, and similar Wellsian exercises in prognostication. In the novel Professor Ernest Keppel dismisses Dr. Holdman Stedding's *Utopias and Visions of the Future* (SB, 170) in terms echoing critical reactions to *The Food of the Gods* and *A Modern Utopia*. Cited specifically is the priggish, uncharming nature of, as it were, "rather absurdly dressed celluloid dolls living on tabloids in a glass lavatory" (SB, 171). And in Joseph Davis' repudiation of his successful career as a popular historian who optimistically emphasized the benevolent development of human life over the ages, lies Wells's self-conscious challenge to various notions expressed or implied in *The Outline of History*.

Wells, it is important to reiterate, repudiates less than he revises, seeking to derive from the preparatory experimentation of his earlier years (1898 to 1920, the significant terminal date) a greater synthesis of his thought and his art. Unlike the Martians in *The War of the Worlds* and somewhat similar to the Master Spirit from Mars in *The Autocracy of Mr. Parham*, the aliens in *Star Begotten* remain unseen, are indeed only hypothetical; the power they possess to transform humanity into a more advanced state is less threatening than promising finally, so that the very concept of "invasion" is inverted in the later novel. Unlike *The Food of the Gods* and *A Modern Utopia*, *Star Begotten* presents only an abstract configuration of the future resulting from this possible benign invasion: "the trouble is that we have no material in our minds out of which we can build a concrete vision of things to come. How can we see or feel the future until we have made the future and are actually there?" (SB, 172). Unlike *The Outline of History*, the vague future predicted in *Star Begotten* is not the product of linear growth but of linear-like expansive parallel development, of the emergence of a more encompassing alternate possibility at once contingent upon yet distinct from the human past. This paradox, a later manifestation of Wells's notion of opposite idea as signifying essential complement rather than antithesis and of time as a fourth dimension, informs every level of *Star Begotten*. It is typically embodied in Davis' dreams, which take "him into a world where our ideas of form and process, of space and time, are no longer valid. In his dreams it was not as if he went across space to Mars, it was as if a veil became translucent" (SB, 103). And it generates the debate running through the novel concerning whether the emerging new species of humanity is a fresh start or an evolutionary advance within *Homo sapiens*.

Frustrating reader expectations, the novel never resolves this debate, offering at best a synthetic view of process as a condition in which everyone "is always beginning" (SB, 196). The novel suggests that *Homo sideralis*, the hypothetical species derived from the genetic changes effected by the alien-directed cosmic rays, is somehow simultaneously a biological sport and an evolutionary development within *Homo sapiens* (SB, 49); the two species are no more opposed than are spirit and matter, reality and dream—in neither of which are the two apparent oppositions mutually exclusive (SB, 107, 183):

There is this secondary world which has worked its way into language everywhere, a sort of fold in the membrane that has established itself in a thousand metaphors, got itself most unwarrantably taken for granted by nearly everybody. Other-worldliness, the idea of a ghost world, a spirit world, side by side with actuality. It overlaps and lies beside reality, like it and yet different; a parody of it done in phantoms; a sort of fuddled overlap; a universe of imaginary emanations, the consequence of a con-genital squint. Beside every man we see his spirit—which is really there—beside the universe we imagine a Great Spirit. Whenever the mental going is a bit hard, whenever our intellectual eyes feel the glare of truth, we lose focus and slither off into Ghostland. Ghostland is half-way to dreamland, where *all* rational checks are lost. In Ghostland, that world of the spirit, you can find unlimited justifications for your impulses; un-limited evasions from rational obligation. That's my main charge against the human mind; this persistent confusing dualism. The last achievement of the human mind is to see life simply and see it whole. (SB, 155-156)

Just as *Homo sapiens* is comprised of body and mind, which appear con-trary but which are requisite to human nature, *Homo sideralis* embodies continuity and departure in that he joins "bodies fit for earth" and Martian minds (SB, 52). *Homo sideralis* is "a sort of half-breed" (SB, 143), a "new creature" extending and at the same time departing from the past of *Homo sapiens* (SB, 144, 195). Just as the new genetic change will occur within human cells, just as the Martian brain will be housed in the terrestrial human body, just as mind exists within flesh or spirit resides within matter, *Homo sideralis* will evolve within *Homo sapiens.* Such argument by analogy implies that *Homo sideralis* is indeed "integral to this scheme of space and time" (SB, 183).

Like *Homo sideralis, Star Begotten* combines something old and some-thing new. It has adopted the concepts of a Martian invasion, of prog-nostication, and of progress as presented by Wells from 1898 to 1920 for the purpose of modifying expectations generated by them to the extent that even the terror associated with the idea of an alien invasion is trans-formed into a hypothetical benign advent. In contrast to *The War of the Worlds,* this novel offers no real plot, no solution or real conclusion, not even the certainty that an invasion is truly underway. And Wells is also careful to indicate that the entire notion of the genetic mutation of *Homo sapiens* in the novel is both original and antiquated, is in fact an adapta-tion of one of humanity's most well-known and cherished stories: the biblical Christmas account.

In accord with a characteristic Wellsian procedure, emanating from the view that "for ages human life has been playing much the same tune with variations" (SB, 61)—hence "always beginning"—Joseph Davis is a contemporary manifestation of the type exemplified by the New Testament Joseph, Son of David: "Since his school days he had had a secret detestation of his own Christian name. Facetious upper school boys had made it plain that there was a shadow on it. Neither in the Old Testament nor in the New, is the name Joseph adorned with that halo of triumphant virility which is the desire of every young male" (SB, 36-37). Of Davis's wife Mary, Dr. Stedding says, "There is not a painted Madonna in all the world with a lovelier bambino than hers" (SB, 100). And the novel concludes with Joseph and Mary's mutual realization that they are "star begotten" and that the future of *Homo sideralis* is centered in their Christ-like child: "Never . . . had anything in the world so calmly and steadfastly resolved to assert its right to think and act in its own way in its own time" (SB, 199).

By demythologizing biblical types, and in the process depicting contemporary experience as a more broadly realized parallel dimension of the biblical narrative to be always more fully expanding in time, Wells confronts and "exorcises" reader expectations generated by these types. Wells even intimates that the biblical account of the Nativity is something of a prototypical science-fiction story. In contrast to the New Testament, *Star Begotten* focusses upon the parents, particularly Joseph, rather than upon the special child. This outcome was perhaps foreshadowed in the earlier refusal to depict priggish celluloid dolls. The Davis child, in whom a divinelike Martian mentality is presumably incarnated in human flesh, may be one of those "strange exceptional figures" who "every now and then [appear] in history" (SB, 64). Actually he symbolizes every child anywhere on earth, in each of whom "the world is being born again," is "always beginning" (SB, 192, 196). Potentiality for the transformation of humanity into more encompassing parallel dimensions of existence lies within every child. But since, *contra* the example of *A Modern Utopia*, a "concrete vision of things to come" cannot be rendered, Wells emphasizes the parents of the child, people living in the reader's dimension of reality and responsible for the education of the next generation.[18]

Moreover, Wells ends his novel with the birth of the parents' self-awareness very shortly after the appearance of their child, in contrast to the New Testament version (especially according to Matthew), which begins with the birth of the Christ beneath the star in the East and details the career of the Messiah. *Star Begotten*, in short, remains unfinished, the promise of its title apparently unfulfilled. It records a moment in the reader's realm of experience that inclines towards some more encompassing dimension of possibility, a moment in an ongoing process of presumably infinite range. In this sense the novel is a mere prologue, especially when compared to the New Testament account. The novel points beyond its tentative ending and away from itself as a self-contained text—an effect reinforced in fact by its biblical analogue and its allusions to earlier Wellsian works—to the world of the reader, whom the parents typify. Ideally, in Wells's view, the reader is to experience a birth of self-awareness concerning his own prospects as a parent, in the broadest sense, every one of whose children is potentially "starbegotten."

Ideally the reader should ascertain that just as Mary and Joseph Davis, like their biblical prototypes, are the people *within* or behind the event of the remarkable birth and just as the birth itself is the product of a genetic change *within* human cells amounting to the incarnation of Martian mind *within* human flesh, so too the dimension of human reality that is *Homo sideralis* lies veiled (SB, 103) *within* each reader. By demystifying the biblical account of Joseph and Mary, Wells lifts the veil of Christian mythology and reveals a greater dimension of contemporary reality within their story. This demystification includes as well an "opening out," an unveiling or broadening, of audience expectations concerning a Wellsian work of science-fiction and of prognostication.[19] The reader's anticipation of conventions in Wells's work are, in short, revised; like Joseph Davis, the reader "pass[es] from a hunt for monsters to an investigation of outstanding endowment, to the detection and analysis of what is called genius in every field of human activity" (SB, 101).

Star Begotten is a science-fiction novel which has undergone a genetic change, a modification from *within* the genre. Like Joseph Davis, it simultaneously incorporates a distinctive individuality and an enlarged or revised generic typicality. Similarly to *Homo sideralis'* incarnation of Martian brain within human flesh, this novel exhibits the new, expanded, more clarified (less veiled) mentality of Wells in the Thirties, a mentality "incarnated" within the invasion formula utilized in his early science fiction, specifically *The War of the Worlds*. Indeed Wells's very example underscores his message that *Homo sideralis* exists potentially as a dimension within all humanity, for the description of the mutated species' mind as a "simpler, clearer and more powerful way of thinking" (SB, 139) echoes Wells's remarks pertaining to what he believed had occurred within his own mind after 1920. He was still H. G. Wells, even as *Star Begotten* was still a science-fiction novel; but this novel, like its author, also displayed a newness, a broadened dimension (expansively parallel, not strictly linear, in relation to its predecessors) implying an open-ended form rich in possibility for apparently countless new ideological and fictional beginnings, each expressive of an evolutionary advance toward the ideal science-fiction novel.

Like that of *The Autocracy of Mr. Parham*, *The Croquet Player*, and *The Camford Visitation*, then, the structure of *Star Begotten* is subtly managed by Wells to elicit expectations in the reader concerning such matters as plot and closure. These anticipations are in turn frustrated and revised (for the purpose of installing new ideological and artistic possibilities suggested by the text) by finally existing outside the text and in the world of the reader. This subtle management in *Star Begotten* includes the narrative voice, which (in contrast to Wells's experiments with it in the 1920's) is left unagitated and unreflexive, even as in the novel the body of *Homo sapiens* is left intact during the alleged invasion of the Martians. Mutated is the genelike "ideological framework" (SB, 153) arising from within the cell-like or bodylike conventions of the Bible and of such science-fiction novels of alien invasion as *The War of the Worlds*. Like *Homo sideralis*, *Star Begotten* is a half-breed work. It is for Wells a new species of science-fiction novel, at once continuous with his early science fiction and distinct from it, simultaneously traditional or typical (the biblical analogue) and innovative or individual (the ideas carried by the vehicular analogue). The ideological framework of the novel is never complete or capable of yielding narrative closure, "always beginning" as new ideas expanding pregnantly within old structures. The ideological framework of the novel constitutes the "new, simpler, clearer and more powerful way of thinking" embodied in Wells's fictional artistry during the 1930's. This framework reflects the multidimensional framework of the human mind. The structural open-endedness and "realism" of *Star Begotten* suggested to Wells the capacity of the science-fiction genre to accommodate countless beginnings as each new clarifying ideological framework within such works generates from within itself successive enlargements of parallel dimensions of human possibility. In its demonstration of generic flexibility, *Star Begotten* was, for Wells, a new species of fiction, typically continuous with his early work while at the same time a distinctive revision contributing to an evolutionary asymptotic advancement towards the ultra-science-fiction novel.

CHAPTER IV

The Womb of Time

Anyone familiar with critical reactions to Wells's late fiction is likely to experience difficulty in approaching *Brynhild* (1937) and *Apropos of Dolores* (1938) expectantly. These two novels have been shunted aside as insignificant works mirroring their author's preference for explicit pronouncement rather than for the artistic embodiment of ideas. If not passed over completely in recent commentary, they tend to be dismissed rapidly with such observations as that *Dolores* expresses Wells's revenge on Odette Keun and *Brynhild* "gives the impression of a man rummaging in the attic of his memory, taking out old ideas and plots, and dusting them off for the last time."[1] Even in the year of its publication *Brynhild* received a painful reception, its one very favorable review offset by a vicious mock-interview concerning the book.[2] And *Dolores* at best received a dubious response, one reviewer praising it as the best novel Wells had written in years, two others appreciating the portrait of the narrator, and a host of others complaining of dullness, poor characterization, obtuseness, and unintentional humor.[3]

Most reviewers then, like many critics today, remained insensitive to the aesthetic quality of these two novels, which are particularly noteworthy in documenting the maturation of Wells's artistry. They receive separate treatment here from the other works of their period, discussed in the last chapter, because they are rich texts disclosing the deeper range of Wells's technique of the splintering frame. In these two novels Wells reinforced the technique of the splintering frame by adapting various philosophic views, most notably modified Schopenhauerian and Spenglerian concepts.

The two in-depth readings which follow are by no means exhaustive. They are designed to explore specifically two adapted philosophic overviews germane to Wells's technique of the splintering frame. In fact a wealth of other modified philosophical strands contribute to the artistic range of Wells's late fiction. Some of these—e.g., Hegelian dialectic and the Nietzschean Superman—have been previously mentioned in passing. Much work awaits to be done on these related subjects, but for now this chapter seeks to enlarge our discussions of Wells's artistic achievement by stressing two instances of how Wells modified ("advanced," in his view) the thought of two men to lend substantive ideological support to his artistic management of the splintering frame in his fiction.

Schopenhauer, Maori Symbolism, and *Brynhild*

The reader of *Brynhild* might first be struck by its spare, old-fashioned story of the breakdown of a marriage and of a consequent brief affair involving the wife, who struggles for a degree of self-awareness and identity.[4] This is all that happens in *Brynhild*. The novel commences in the middle of the night with Rowland Palace, an author egotistically worrying about his public image, and with Brynhild Palace, his wife of nine years, trying to comfort him. The story really concerns Brynhild's deepening consciousness, in counterpoint to her husband's increasing lust for popularity. While at a weekend party at a lush estate, Brynhild meets Alfred Bunter, an imaginative poet who is a fugitive from the law and who has a brief affair with her. By the end of the novel Bunter is gone and Brynhild is pregnant with his child, a fact she never tells the poet.

Wells maintained that art should depict life in all its mundaneness, and the plot of *Brynhild* is no exception to this rule. Wells also believed that beneath the surface of life's particulars startling discoveries await, and so he designed the commonplace plot of Brynhild to reveal, through the technique of the splintering frame, a greater pattern of reality within the phenomena of mundane existence. As the subtitle *The Show of Things* intimates, the novel concerns modes of perception of reality, a theme embodied in the characters, imagery, and structure of the work.

In order to appreciate the interrelation of these three features of the book it is useful to recognize two clues given in the work. The first appears early when the narrative voice refers to "Schopenhauer's realization of the importance of Show (*Vorstellung*)" (Bry, 23). A careful reading of *Brynhild* discloses that modified Schopenhauerian notions provide a philosophical basis for its artistic effects. The standard English translation of *Die Welt als Wille und Vorstellung* appeared in 1883, seeing numerous editions through the turn of the century. Wells claimed familiarity with this translation (EA, 656), apparently read the extensive section on Schopenhauer in Will Durant's *The Story of Philosophy* (1927) (AF, 12, 75; YC, 288), and in a revised edition of *The Outline of History* (1927) referred to the "profound and penetrating speculations" of Schopenhauer (OH, 995). However, there is no way to know how much of the German philosopher's work Wells read, how much he learned about it from secondary sources, or how much of what was encountered he understood accurately. Such concerns provide a proper cautionary note without undermining a sensitivity to the influence of Schopenhauer on *Brynhild*, which exhibits enough similarities to the thought of the German philosopher to warrant comparison. Indeed, as the subtitle of the novel and the specific reference to *Vorstellung* suggest, deep philosophical issues at least similar to those of Schopenhauer lie beneath the surface of the novel's apparently mundane plot.

Modified Schopenhauerian thought provides a philosophical basis for the structure of *Brynhild*. But Wells's experiment with structure in this novel required a concrete illustration of the abstract remarks about art in *The World as Will and Idea*, and he found that example in Ettie A. Rout's *Maori Symbolism* (1926), to which he refers, as a second clue, in the penultimate paragraph of *Brynhild*:

> In New Zealand, as Mrs. Ettie (Rout) Hornibrook showed so ably and interestingly in her *Maori Symbolism*, the decorations on a beam or a pillar may be expanded by an understanding imagination into the most complete and interesting of patterns, and so it is with this book. It is a novel in the Maori style, a presentation of imaginative indications. (Bry, 302)

By adapting the manner of Maori archetypes or sacred symbols, Wells attempted to give *Brynhild* a structure appropriate to the qualified Schopenhauerian ideas also informing its imagery and characterization.

Only four characters dominate Wells's novel: Rowland and Brynhild Palace, representing refined society, and Immanuel Cloote and Alfred Bunter, representing the lower levels of society. Save for Brynhild, they are types, and it is quite true, as one critic has observed, that Cloote is Rowland's alter ego and Bunter is Brynhild's secret.[5] But this relationship signifies much more. Cloote and Rowland belong, as it were, to one species of the human race, whereas Bunter and Brynhild belong to another. The fundamental difference between these two species lies in the will.

The concept of will is central to the meaning of *Brynhild*. It is easy to mistake a particular character's view of it for Wells's. For instance, Brynhild speculates, rather unfashionably by today's standards, on the possibility that "the will of a woman is different from a man's" (Bry, 185; italics deleted), that while the male will is initiating and aggressive the female will is resistant and responsive. In fact, however, Brynhild's subsequent experiences enlarge these ideas, and we, as readers, should perceive that difference in wills is not sexually determined. Rather divergence in the exercise of will seems more indicative of two distinct kinds of human beings, found in both sexes as well as at all levels of society, a conclusion to be reiterated in *Apropos of Dolores*.

Rowland Palace possesses an aggressive will, expressed in an egotistic desire (satirized in the novel) to maniplate others. Immanuel Cloote, Palace's public relations man, shares in this endeavor as a "secret agent" (Bry, 99). Together they strive to manage Rowland's image in terms of the "show," presentation, *Vorstellung* of life. In contrast, Brynhild and Bunter possess essentially passive wills. Unlike her husband, who smugly seeks to fortify "the façade he presented to the world," Brynhild inquires "into all the neglected possibilities that might be pining and fretting behind the façade she had hitherto unquestioningly supposed to be herself" (Bry, 24). As her self-awareness increases, she discovers she is "passive," enjoys "watch[ing] other people," and manifests an apparent "lack of will" (Bry, 132, 178). Bunter, for whom Brynhild feels deep sympathy, likewise manifests a "detached interest" (Bry, 105) in the "show" of life, does not relish surfaces or "how things look" (Bry, 217). Bunter is characterized by the same passivity of will Brynhild had initially attributed only to women. That difference in will is one of human kind, not of sex or class, is reinforced when Bunter relates in some detail the story of his second marriage. "She [his second wife] seduced me," the passively-willed, responsive Bunter explains in prelude to his description of Freda's egotism and desire to "show-off" before an audience (Bry, 224-226), behavior rather similar to Rowland Palace's.

This distinction between two kinds of will can be illuminated in light of Schopenhauer's ideas about this faculty. In *The World as Will and Idea* Schopenhauer stresses, in accord with the Oriental influences on his thought, the distinction between the world of phenomena as *Maya* (illusion) and the world within ourselves as reality; to pass through "the single narrow door to the truth," he explains, "we must learn to understand nature from ourselves, not conversely ourselves from nature."[6] The difference is a matter of will. For Schopenhauer, who is not completely consistent in his use of the term, the will is an unconscious, blind, incessant impulse, the inner nature of everything that lives, the "endless striving" behind all human desires (I, 213, 364; cf. Bry, 43). It is objectified in bodily actions (cf. Bry, 49), which to some extent conceal even as they reveal the true identity of the will "as the thing in itself" constituting "the inner, true, and indestructible nature of man" (II, 411). We do not move the will (as in Cartesian thought), rather will is greater than and primary to intellect. Awareness of the reality of the will emerges piece-meal and *a posteriori*, as our intellect assesses our actions and reactions (II, 421). Those who fail to realize this underying, *internal* truth about the unitary will live on the surface (*Maya*) of life and delude themselves with a sense of personal distinctness separate from and better than that of others. Living in the world in terms of the *principium individuationis*, these people egotistically seek their own gratification at the expense of others (I, 455), who seem less real; hence the origin of so much misery in the world. Believing, either consciously or unconsciously, that "the essence of success is personality, that is to say *individual distraction*" (Bry, 87), Rowland, Cloote and Freda manifest the egotism and impul-siveness of the blind will at its worst. The consequences of their behavior are, in the context of Wells's novel, at once ludicrous and tragic.

Good action, in Schopenhauer's view, requires liberation, insofar as it is possible, from the perception of and attachment to the world as pheno-mena, or "show." Through self-knowledge we can *approach* awareness of the noumenal reality within phenomenal particularity and multiplicity. Through conscious disinterest in the surface of existence one can arrest egoism, suppress individuality. Through this more passive disposition the disinterested person recognizes that all beings lie "as near to him as his own person lies to the egoist" (I, 489): "all true and pure love is sym-pathy, and all love which is not sympathy is selfishness. *Eros* is selfishness, *agape* is sympathy" (I, 485). The passive "state of voluntary renuncia-tion, resignation, true indifference and perfect will-lessness" (I, 490) characterizes the ideal human disposition. This is the condition *approxi-mated*—Wells does not fully endorse the Schopenhauerian implications of the passive will—by Bunter and Brynhild, whose mutual awareness of "universal desire . . . universal frustration" unites them in a "secret col-laboration" (Bry, 134, 266). In response to the "unsatisfied cravings" of life (Bry, 218), they mutually resign themselves to their uncertain destinies.

Schopenhauer eventually argues for a mystical detachment from the world, for an ultimate negation and withdrawal whereby (somehow) the will turns upon itself (III, 430-431). Wells apparently knew this feature of Schopenhauer's thought, for the narrative voice of the novel speaks of Brynhild's "new half-mystical self-devotion to the physical rebirth of our world" (Bry, 301). The novel emphasizes the physical world finally in a way distinct from Schopenhauer. For Wells, Schopenhauer's willful egoist and will-less saint typify two species of the human race. Both manifest something like a Collective Will—Schopenhauer speaks similarly when

91

he defines the will as that which constitutes the inner nature of everything. For Wells, only those with a passive will are constructively attuned. Attunement means serving instrumentally (not by intent but by conscious resignation) in the evolution of humanity. Brynhild and Bunter are two representatives of a different and emergent species of mankind. In renouncing the surface of life they perceive the interior reality of existence; that is to say, they experience the Collective Will in themselves. They do not rationally understand, indeed hardly recognize "the supreme mystery" (Bry, 50) which they serve, any more than does Rowland, who uses this phrase to describe his own role in life and who also believes rightly, for the wrong reasons, that "the noumenon is forever unknown" (Bry, 91). The noumenon may be Nothing, and it is certainly not a deity; whatever it is, Brynhild, at least, does intuit something of its reality during her pregnancy as the "juices in her blood that had taken possession of her, and filled her with this deep irrational satisfaction, had a very imperious suggestion about them of being real" (Bry, 300). The human will, as it participates in something like a Collective will, remains a mystery. But for Wells, in contrast to Schopenhauer, the force of that will does not appear to be aimless. Wells shares Schopenhauer's view of the world as illusion, suffering and frustration (Bry, 218), but he does not endorse the German philosopher's final pessimism. For Wells the split between noumenon (interior) and phenomena (exterior) is not eternal; in accord with Christian tradition and suggested by his technique of the splintering frame, Wells believes in the possibility of ringing in the kingdom through the slow, evolutionary conversion of interior ideality into external reality. So Brynhild through her children and Bunter through his writings voluntarily yield their wills to fate and give birth to internal truth made manifest in the world.

The optimism in *Brynhild*, one should remark, is most modest. Even in the final line of the novel proper—"If indeed there was in human experience as yet any such thing as reality" (Bry, 300)—the simply stated *as yet* hardly balances the overall implied dubiety of the other words. The fragility of this optimism is reflected as well in Bunter's expression of a desperate hope that "somehow, some day we will get the better of this predestinate world" (Bry, 268). Brynhild and Bunter receive intuitive *a posteriori* intimations of their place in some vague universal scheme, but they never consciously fathom the mystery in which they are playing so crucial a role. (This point is reinforced in the novel by a satiric presentation of a game of charades [during the weekend party] in which the participants know only the letter they represent but not the word to which they contribute [Bry, 119-120]). Brynhild's and Bunter's intimations of this mystery, as the narrative voice tells us, is "half-mystical."

Before specifically considering the structure of *Brynhild*, it is useful to relate Schopenhauer's understanding of art to Maori symbolism. For Schopenhauer, art should not exist for its own sake but should express the noumenal mystery informing the will. The artist contemplates this reality behind phenomena, and his art conveys knowledge of it through Platonic ideas, through essential forms of archetypes supplanting a reader's experience of individuality in himself and in the world. Art communicates "aesthetic" knowledge (I, 271; III, 180), something "felt" intuitively, rather than comprehended rationally, of the mystery of existence.

Similar concepts apparently characterize Maori symbolism. In her study Ettie A. Rout indicates that the New Zealand Maori artist rejects the notion of "Art for Art's sake" and strives to render an "expression of ideas and principles" true to human experience.[7] This same view informs Wells's approach to art, as is most evident in his well-known controversy with Henry James. Moreover, Wells went further; "if the novel is to follow life it must be various and discursive," he announced, "life is diversity and entertainment, not completeness and satisfaction." Lack of satisfaction, for Schopenhauer as well, is the chief attribute of life; of necessity this lack is reflected in the work of an artist. Similarly the crude-looking designs of the Maori artist convey an impression of incompleteness. But just as the archetype in Schopenhauerian art objectifies the mysterious hidden reality (will) behind phenomena, each sacred symbol of the Maori artist provides the "foundation of the pattern, and a key to its inner meaning[;] but its inner meaning was to be secret, except to certain members of the nobility entrusted with the preservation of this inner meaning as Sacred Knowledge (cf. the Mysteries of Egyptian priests and others)."[8]

Such notions, or very similar ones, inform *Brynhild*. They in fact dictate the satiric treatment of Rowland Palace in the novel. As a member of the upper class of society, Rowland maintains that he is "one of the great company that served the supreme mystery" (Bry, 50). In a certain sense he is correct, insofar as (in Schopenhauerian terms) everyone is driven by will; but by asserting his will as ego and by substituting the "show" of life for his art, Rowland is in bad faith in his duty to serve the supreme mystery. In fact he makes his phenomenal self its own end, hence displacing his service to noumenal reality; and he hires Cloote to be, as it were, the priest of the self. Wells has tremendous fun with Cloote, who sees himself as Rowland's Aaron, his John the Baptist (Bry, 95). Priestlike Cloote exhibits a magical and "strange hypnotic manner" (Bry, 159, 289), appears to write in hieroglyphics (Bry, 278)[9] and uses such expressions as "*Saecula Saeculorum*" (Bry, 281; cf. p. 47). Cloote's activity as a public relations man parodies the sacred priestly duty of the artist.

Whereas Rowland worships himself, Alfred Bunter seeks to hide his identity. Art is sacred to Bunter, whose work (like Schopenhauerian and Maorian art) expresses ideas intimating a reality beneath the phenomena of life. In contrast to the exhibition of restraint and order in Rowland's work (Bry, 5, 64), Bunter's art conveys a "rude vigor" (Bry, 62), an impulsiveness, uncertainty, unnevenness, and lack of finish reflecting the reality (Collective Will) he intuitively senses to exist within the phenomenal world. These same features apply to *Brynhild* as a work of art.

Brynhild gives the appearance of an elaborate fragment. It opens at seventeen minutes past three in the morning, covers less than a year, and closes before the issues raised are resolved. The entire novel gives a *surface* impression of an overdone prologue; and it is, in this sense, understandable that some reviewers complained vehemently about the seemingly abrupt ending of the novel.[10] Wells deliberately violates fictional convention in this instance, leaving the reader dissatisfied and, we might add, as "expectant" as is pregnant Brynhild. The product of Wells's splintering frame technique, this very discontent generates cognitive processes in the reader by involving the reader in the Schopenhauerian concerns of the novel, particularly the experience of the frustration generated by ceaseless human desires.

Even the seemingly tacked-on, two-page "Envoy" resolves little. It commences by dismissing itself—"Sufficient unto the novel is the story thereof" (Bry, 301)—then proceeds in a resigned, even disinterested tone to deflate any romantic notions the reader might hold concerning Brynhild and Bunter. We are told that Brynhild remains married to Rowland, their continued incompatability a mere fact, and that she once more later in life met Bunter "with an entirely unromantic friendliness—and no revelations" (Bry, 302). And Wells's novel denies revelations to the superficial reader conditioned by tidy narrative endings and by fictional conventions in general, at least as Wells perceived them. By means of this denial *Brynhild* involves the reader in the text, achieves a fourth dimension (reader relativity), and generates a form more intimated than achieved.

As Wells's reference to Maori art indicates, there is a pattern concealed, as it were, by the "decorations" of the plot of the novel. In Maori carving "the artists frequently halved the original design [one thinks immediately of the truncated effect of *Brynhild*], repeating the halved form in different ways for friezes"; "the original design has been disguised by flowers, tendrils, feathers, etc., but the *motif* is seen readily when these composite designs are resolved to their elemental lines."[11] These motifs are, in Schopenhauerian and Maorian terms, archetypes objectifying ultimate ideas or mysteries.

In *Brynhild* this "secret" archetype is the eddy. An eddy is a backwardly-circling current of water, or whirlpool; figuratively it means turning aside or departing from the main current of thought. It can be imaged as a spiral—a plane curve formed by a point that moves around a fixed center (the will, in Schopenhauerian terms) and that continually increases its distance from it. In *Brynhild* it serves as an emblem of Wells's notion of the spiral of time (remarked in Chapter One), but is also an archetypal image repeated often in Maori carvings (it appears countlessly in Rout's book) and, incidentally, in the art of the Orient influencing Schopenhauer's thought. Correspondent to the literal and figurative meaning of *eddy*, water imagery is associated with thought throughout *Brynhild*. Rowland, for instance is at one point said to be "launched upon a wide and congenial flow of thought. . . . as if the dam penning up some great reservoir of imaginations had given way" (Bry, 34; cf. the image applied to Bunter, [Bry, 228]); and Brynhild's thoughts appear to be "as deep and unfathomable as the depths of her dark eyes" (Bry, 44). Rowland wishes to live in a "great flow of self-expression" (Bry, 43), but his wife finds her thoughts to be "as shapeless . . . as things peered at in an overshadowed pool" (Bry, 44). The image of the pool, again associated with Brynhild at the end of the novel (Bry, 298), is (especially in terms of ripples) interchangeable in the book with the image of an eddy. Brynhild fears that she continually "spin[s] round and round . . . ideas," that she time and again merely "get[s] back to the old eddy" (Bry, 193, 207):

> She was caught in that eddy. She was just spinning round in that eddy while the stream of life was flowing by. The eddy was flatter than it used to be but it held her just the same. And there was no prospect, no open door at least, of escape from this futile circling. (Bry, 169)

Brynhild resists her experience of whirlpool-like backward-circling because she mistakenly draws an analogy between it and "the chief entertainments in the Great Fair of Life" that circulate "faster and faster" only to return "in each case to the point of departure" (Bry, 169). She and Bunter deplore what they perceive as an endless recapitulation: the tyranny of determinism, predestination, the plot of history.[12] As Bunter expresses the dilemma: "We jump out of bed [as if to start over] and right away we stumble over our stale selves of the day before" (Bry, 209).

Both misread this experience, even as Brynhild initially misattributes difference in will to sexual distinctions—a clever Wellsian touch confuting the tendency of readers and reviewers to identify an author's view with that of his protagonist. She is not, as she thinks, precisely "where she had started" (Bry, 200); for, as her father explained to her when she was a child, "Everything goes round, my dear, and comes back—a little different—a very little different—but it comes back" (Bry, 170). To be caught in an eddy of thought, Wells's novel indicates, is to be very slowly *edified* or enlightened about reality. This sense of eddy is both a modification of Schopenhauer's view of our inability to change the fundamental character of human existence and a microcosmic illustration of the evolutionary motion of the macrocosmic spiral of time. Edifying thought expands consciousness, even as the spire image of an eddy depicts a curve increasingly expanding from its center (Schopenhauer's will).[13] In contrast is the linear-appearing sweep of the life lived by Rowland, Cloote, and Freda; all three hate "to be self-conscious" (Bry, 3) and prefer the illusion of progress (the final chapter is ironically entitled "Mr. Rowland Palace Goes Upward and On"). In turning aside from the main flow of things Brynhild becomes increasingly self-aware. In Schopenhauerian terms, she receives intimations of the reality behind the external world by encountering that reality (will, center of the eddy) within herself. In Wellsian terms she participates in an evolutionary progress whereby mankind very gradually closes with an interior ideal human existence; she passively participates in the spiral of time, the expanding process of which splinters the frame of external, or phenomenal, existence so that an interior ideal humanity might steadily emerge.

Of the several ways one can trace the small changes in Brynhild, the most interesting involves Wells's management of the motif of motherhood associated with her. At the start of the novel she is depicted as Rowland's surrogate mother, who sometimes feels "a desire to spank him hard and good" (Bry, 16) as if he were a petulant child deserving reproof; instead she provides patient maternal support: "I'll come up with you and smooth your pillow and uncrumple your sheets and put you to sleep"

(Bry, 22). The motif appears subtly several times in the course of the novel (e.g., Bry, 46-47, 247-248, 258), until at its close Brynhild is carrying Bunter's child. Her maternity is itself pregnant with significance, for she is now dedicated "to the physical rebirth of [the] world" (Bry, 301). In a way, then, the entire novel has been an eddy; it has, at its conclusion, circled back upon its beginning. Brynhild remains married to Rowland, her relationship with him has not on the surface changed, and her primary role is still maternal. But, as her father told her, very small changes occur in the experience of circling; and the eddylike development, or splintering frame, of the novel shows, what Brynhild herself barely sees, that recapitulation is accompanied by slow expansion, that underneath the illusion of appearances, her role and her relationship with Rowland are not quite the same as they were less than a year ago. They have "evolved."

Bunter too must start over by giving up his assumed identity and returning to his past, so that his presence in the novel concludes at the very point where his story begins—the trouble with his second wife. The "Envoy" alludes obliquely to subsequent vague changes in him, though on the surface his later resumption of a writer's identity appears to be essentially the same as it was previously (save for a beard). But, more importantly, Bunter's role in the novel contributes to its eddylike structure. Bunter serves as a very modified version of the "entrancing Perseus" figure who, in conventional fiction, "restores meaning to life" for the heroine; Brynhild wonders:

> All fiction is full of these fluttering Persei, they are as common there as white butterflies on an early day in summer. They take the initiative. They overcome all your scruples. They do everything for you. It is very misleading to the young. Brynhild could not persuade herself that in real life she had ever so much as glimpsed a specimen. (Bry, 172)

Certainly Bunter is no Perseus of this sort; but, oddly, he does play a somewhat modified version of this typical role. As a fellow spirit and as the father of her child, Bunter has contributed to the "expansion" not only of Brynhild's body but also of her mind. In a sense he has aided Brynhild in terms of an *internal* release or escape, and in doing so he fulfills a conventional fictional role at a covert level. This modification of Bunter's typical role is like the eddy-effect of the alteration in Brynhild's maternal role. Both recapitulate the most mundane events of life and fiction, but like episodes or personality types within the spiral of time (implicit in the eddy image), they do so with small, hardly noticeable changes in the conventions of life and of the novel.

The overall eddy-effect of Brynhild is prepared for and reinforced by the fact that the conventional linear narrative line of the novel is presented satirically, whereas the pool-like, "swollen-out" contemplative sections, reporting Brynhild's thoughts and Bunter's account of his life, are presented straightforwardly. These latter sections represent, as it were, eddies or contemplative backward-circlings in contrast to the rush of events presented in the linear narrative recounting the apparent progress of Rowland and Cloote. These eddies start out small: at first less than three pages of Brynhild's self-reflection (Bry, 22-24), later nearly five pages of thought disrupting the narrative account of the party at Valliant Chevrell (Bry, 105-109), then an entire chapter (Bry, 157-200). By the end of the book this slowly expanding eddy-effect—similar to the repetition of halved Maori sacred symbols in the decorative components of an overall design—includes the entire novel, which expands in meaning through the technique of the splintering frame and in the process circles backwardly upon itself.

The archetypal image of the eddy,[14] predominant among Maori sacred symbols, is the "complete and interesting" pattern beneath the "decorations" and the "imaginative indications" referred to at the end of *Brynhild*. The image of the eddy objectifies the very structure of the novel, giving it a form appropriate to the modified Schopenhauerian concepts reflected in the work, especially the notion of the will as the mysterious generating center of all life. Since it permits diversity or discursive excursions of the sort evident in the novel, the eddylike structure of *Brynhild* satisfies Wells's notion of the novel as various, discursive, and incomplete —like life, in Wells's view. The structure of this novel is a transitional form providing no firm sense of completion or satisfaction for the characters or for the readers, both of whom experience a Schopenhauerian world of frustration. This structure remains as elusive as the transient ripples of an eddy appearing out of and disappearing into nowhere—apparently there in motion before our eyes, but never permanent or quite defined; somewhat *edifying* in their rhythmic expansiveness, but always half-mystically beyond comprehension. Like an eddy, in a figurative sense, *Brynhild* turns aside or departs from the main current of fictional conventions, as Wells saw them. In this process of splintering its frame, it opens outwardly to include the reader in the eddy of thought. It is one of Wells's most remarkable experiments with fictional structure.

Spengler and *Apropos of Dolores*

As good as *Brynhild* is, *Apropos of Dolores* is even better. It manifests Wells's continuing interest in the application of modified Schopenhauerian ideas to his aesthetic theory, but nowhere to the extent evident in *Brynhild*. Rather, in *Dolores* the manifestation of the technique of the splintering frame is primarily reinforced by an adaptation of concepts expressed in Oswald Spengler's *The Decline of the West* (1918), the authorized English translation of which appeared in 1926. Spengler's work exerted a sizeable influence upon many thinkers and writers of the Twenties and Thirties. It reformulated concepts of decadence prevalent during the late nineteenth century, in such works as Max Nordau's extremely popular *Degeneration* (1895), which book reflects attitudes similar to those in Wells's earliest science fiction.[15] At present, the exact degree of Wells's knowledge of Spengler's work remains less certain than his exposure to Schopenhauer's *The World as Will and Idea*. Unlike Schopenhauer, Spengler is barely mentioned in passing in *The Story of Philosophy*, and so Durant's study provides no sure source.

There can be little doubt that Wells disagreed with Spengler on certain issues (BB, 369; AF, 75; HT, 73); he did not share Spengler's assessment of Gothic architecture as the epitomization of Western egotism.[16] He also rejected Spengler's theory of cyclical rise and decline; for, as we have noted, Wells held a notion of time that subsumes cyclical patterns within an evolutionary spiral configuration integrating all pertinent cycles. Spengler may in fact be the target of a reference (made by Wells three years before *Dolores* appeared) to an unidentified historian who engaged in the childish fantasy of analogizing civilizations and individuals in the context of birth and death (NA, 7). Moreover, the *implied* pessimism of Spengler's theory, however much it may have appealed to Wells unconsciously, was not harmonious to Wells's expressed hopefulness during the Thirties. But, typically, whatever exceptions Wells may have taken to Spengler's ideas would not have prevented him from appropriating these concepts for his own use. In fact paralells apparently exist between Wells's and Spengler's views of cyclical patterns in the history of empires.[17] An affinity between these views is suggested as well when the narrator of *The Anatomy of Frustration* bemusedly enquires whether Steele had tried "to out-Spengler Spengler" (AF, 75).

A similar query appears in *Dolores*, when the narrator, Stephen Wilbeck, wonders: "Is this I am discovering here a bit more arbitrary than Spenglerism?" (AD, 177). Yes and no, apparently: "To-night at any rate I am full of my own interpretations," he continues, "You start up your theories and analogies, you hoot like a historian and the facts, the slightly limping facts and striding assumptions, come crowding along" (AD, 177). Earlier Wilbeck remarked how mankind "endures these Spenglers," among others, because "we *have* to endure them. At the worst they are experimentalists in statement" (AD, 169). And Wilbeck very much endures Spengler and the others: "I cannot resist the allurement of these very vulgarities of history I have been denouncing. Suddenly I find my head busy with them, adventitious analogies, wild generalizations, unjustified assertions, fragmentary facts" (AD, 172). He discovers in himself enough thoughts "to fit out a dozen Spenglers" (AD, 177-178), but, significantly, he in fact does much more than endure Spenglerian ideas: "When I thought I was burlesquing those big sociohistorical books I was really adopting a method which allowed an accumulation of ideas below the surface of consciousness to come up to the top in a very convenient manner" (AD, 189).

Such a remark, as we have seen, refers to Wells's revisionist cast of mind during the Thirties. His penchant for inversion, satire, and parody in his early writing had, in his later opinion, been preparatory for the bloom of consciousness, the onset of which he dated as 1920. *Dolores* too refers to this revisionist frame of mind, including an explicit reconsideration of two Wellsian expressions, "a war to end war" and "the salvaging of civilization" (AD, 49, 278).[18] The key word in Wilbeck's remark (quoted above) is *adopting*, referring in the context of the novel to a new species of thought evolving from *within* an older mode of thought. Herein lies not only the significance of the presence of Spenglerian concepts in the novel but also the defining core of the novel's aesthetic achievement. With Spengler's distinction between culture and civilization in mind, Wells viewed his novel as an expression of an emerging culture. By its example *Dolores* indicts the fiction of the Jamesian schools, with its relish for ornament and its implicit defence of art for art's sake, as representative of the state of literature in a declining civilization. Wells discovered in modified Spenglerian concepts a sympathetic philosophical basis for the art he was already practicing, a stimulus urging him in *Dolores* to perhaps the greatest refinement of his literary artistry, particularly his use of the technique of the splintering frame.

Apropos of Dolores is presented as a journal recording the various personal and philosophical thoughts of Stephen Wilbeck, a book publisher who increasingly views his egocentric wife, Dolores, as the embodiment of those forces in life which prevent humanity from achieving happiness.

During most of his narrative Wilbeck engages in leisurely activities and thinks, or deals with embarrassments caused by Dolores and thinks. He begins to believe that Dolores and he represent two different species of the human race. This sense of alienation from Dolores is climaxed in a furious argument during which Dolores accuses Wilbeck of incest with his daughter (Lettice) from his first marriage. Seized by a fit during the argument, Dolores cries out for her pain medicine, which Wilbeck gives her. Later she dies from an overdose, and in his journal Wilbeck confesses his uncertainty about whether he is responsible for her death. After her funeral, Wilbeck eventually extrapolates a philosophical awareness of his and all humanity's complicity in the "probable crime." This journal (the novel) reaches an indefinite end, as Wilbeck interweaves memory and prediction concerning the nature of human existence.

Wilbeck believes that his wife and he represent historical, psychological and evolutionary forces in dialectic. At the historical level, Dolores, typifies the civilization stage of Western culture, as defined by Spengler.[19] According to Spengler, every culture, independent of every other culture, undergoes the organic cycle of birth, growth, decay and death. *Culture* is the word Spengler uses to refer to the vital, creative phase of this cycle; *civilization*, the inevitable subsequent stage, refers to the rigid and cold declining phase of the cycle. A culture attains its apex when it "has actualized the full sum of its possibilities in the shape of peoples, languages, dogmas, arts, states, sciences"; then "the Culture suddenly hardens, it mortifies, its blood congeals, its force breaks down, and it becomes Civilization" (I, 106).

A princess by a previous marriage and formerly "one of the most brilliant women on the Riviera accustomed to *gentlemen*, to men of title, to princes, to men of the world, to unquestioning gallantry," Dolores represents the traditional values of Western civilization (AD, 146, 154). Wilbeck identifies her "traits ... with the warp and woof of history" (AD, 175), especially as manifested in the Spenglerian morphology of history. Typical of the civilization phase she symbolizes, Dolores clings to the past and cannot envision the future; speaking with "the utmost refinement and condescension," she "never forgets," lacks flexibility, and is no longer capable of "a really original thing" (AD, 89, 95, 145, 158). She is increasingly "aggressive" and, as her name suggests, "frequently and abundantly unhappy" (AD, 11, 44); for she personifies the human discontent prevalent in the civilization stages defined by Spengler. Having passed the creative (cultural) phase of her life, she feels "aimless" (AD, 72); and just as civilization, in Spenglerian terms, emphasizes cause and effect, materialism and fads (I, 103-104), so too Dolores self-consciously assigns blame for her melancholy, desires only what is elegant, and uses material objects (especially jewelry and automobiles) as a means of asserting social status (AD, 14, 40, 97, 105). Wilbeck's impression that Dolores tends to transform her lovers into technicians (AD, 152) reinforces her representation of civilization, which, according to Spengler, converts the creative instinct of the cultural phase into systematic behavior stressing the mechanical. Dolores' rigidity, coldness, adherence to form and preoccupation with the past emanate from her fear of decline; she belongs "by nature to a world that is manifestly working out its own destruction by excess of acquisition, assertion and malice" (AD, 228). Her "over-emphasis, her high-pitched voice, her emphatic make-up, her assertive taste in dress," her "blank craving for notice" arise "from some deep doubt in her whether indeed she is really alive" (AD, 73-74, 158). Dolores' sense of personal tragedy issues, as it does in Western civilization as defined by Spengler (I, 130), from a passionate denial of time.

In contrast, Wilbeck represents the creative, cultural phase of a new, different civilization. A member of the proletariat rather than of the leisured nobility typified by Dolores, Wilbeck is free from petrified traditions and enjoys "long, loose, unencumbered activities" (AD, 84). Whereas Dolores is egocentric, aimless and uncreative, Wilbeck is inspired by imagination and humanistic purpose: "I explain and justify myself to myself as a collector and distributor of creative ideas. I have chosen to be the servant of, and a part of, the greater new world that struggles to exist [culture], and not of the old world that is crumbling away [civilization]" (AD, 38-39; cf. 69). Of his relationship with Dolores, he says: "We were profoundly different; that is all. She belonged by nature to a world that is manifestly working out its own destruction by excesses of acquisition, assertion and malice, and I, to the best of my knowledge and belief, belong to a new, less acutely concentrated world that may or may not be able to emerge—wiggle out rather than emerge—from the ruins and survive" (AD, 228). As a spokesman for this new culture, Wilbeck revises an earlier Wellsian idea by advancing the Spenglerian notion that "civilization, as we know it, is not to be salvaged. . . . It comes to an end —it tears and rends into warfare by a senile enlargement of its own traditions" (AD, 278). In opposition to Dolores' old-world "civilized" stress on memory, the past, tragedy, materialism and causality, Wilbeck readily forgets, looks to the future, reflects upon an "innate hopefulness," intuits a transcendental dimension in life and speaks of the mystical core of being (AD, 27, 35, 48, 49, 67, 285)—characteristics of the Spenglerian cultural stage of a civilization. In fact, Dolores' incessant complaints that her husband is "as credulous and changeable as a child," that he "plays" at mending the world, that he seems "a small, pudgy, obstinate, wicked little boy," and that he appears to her as "a stupid child grasping a beautiful toy" (AD, 45, 114, 154, 163, 193) dramatize the Spenglerian concept of the essential childishness of humanity and specifically underscore the infantile stage of the new culture represented by Wilbeck. As Spengler explains, "a Culture is born in the moment when a great soul awakens out of the proto-spirituality of ever-childish humanity, and detaches itself, a form from the formless, a bounded and mortal thing from the boundless and enduring" (I, 106).

Nowhere in *Decline of the West* does Spengler give a more precise explanation of the origin of a culture; as the preceding quotation suggests, Spengler considered the birth of a culture as one of life's mysteries. Wilbeck too shares this viewpoint but also sees leisure as a condition physically and psychologically conducive to the emergence of this culture. According to Foxfield, one of Wilbeck's authors, the increase in mechanization and of a subsequent leisure is dangerous because it gives rise to "the mass unsettlement of the workers," who will turn against the ruling class exemplified by Dolores (AD, 33-34). Wilbeck, who (like Brynhild) makes "discoveries through relaxation" and derives insight through the "lazy activity" of his mind (AD, 11, 189), agrees with Foxfield that mechanization indeed necessitates leisure and that for many this condition proves painful; for some, "the ache of impotent leisure" will prevail and, like Dolores, these people will be "at a loss to find something to do" (AD, 39, 185). But Foxfield's presaged "Age of Miserable Leisure" will not be a "universal tragedy" insofar as it also occasions the birth of new cultures; indeed, Wilbeck explains further (applying an image from Hegel that Wells might have found in Durant's *The Story of Philosophy*),[20] "there are as good worlds in the womb of time as ever came out of it" (AD, 39). Accordingly, when Dolores (Western civilization) dies, Wilbeck (an arising culture) experiences "a state of extreme inactivity" and for a while he does "not know what to do" with himself: "I have been so accustomed for the past thirteen years to subordinate my movements to the aggressions of Dolores that I seem to have lost the power of entirely spontaneous movement altogether" (AD, 205, 209). Shortly, however, as a result of the ache of leisure Wilbeck creates, and eventually he concludes that such "unavoidable leisure" might transform anyone into an author (AD, 221). Whereas initially he felt inert "like a stone," he comes to "feel rather more like a new-laid egg" expectant with possibilities similar to those of the burgeoning culture he represents (AD, 215). Leisure sets the stage for individual psychological adjustment to external changes resulting from the decline of Western civilization as well as to a related internal metamorphosis issuing from the interaction of the components of the self.

Wilbeck's notions about the psychology of the self blend together Freudian and Spenglerian ideas. He refers to Freud's basic trinity of id, ego and superego as ego, heart and intellect, respectively. Wilbeck uses the word *ego*, as Spengler uses it, to refer to the principle trait of Western civilization; as Spengler remarks, "the entire Faustian [Western] ethic, from Thomas Aquinas to Kant, is an 'excelsior'—fulfilment of an 'I' by faith and works . . . and, lastly and supremely, immortality of the 'I' " (I, 309). Symbolizing Western civilization, self-centered Dolores displays a "devouring insatiable egotism"; she is the "human being stripped down to its bare egotism," a type (like Rowland Palace) "so completely individualized . . . that she lacked a distinctive individuality" (AD, 158, 159, 164-165). Like declining Western civilization, Dolores cannot adjust, and for her leisure presents a painful void making her life seem aimless.

Because egotism is "the foundation stuff of humanity" (AD, 159), Wilbeck also experiences self-centered impulses. As the spokesman for a new culture, however, Wilbeck detects within himself a purpose and direction similar to that provided by the Freudian superego. Wilbeck's culture, unlike Dolores' Western civilization, represses egoism. "I am not wholly an ego, and she is," Wilbeck writes, "there is a certain good in me that she has not" (AD, 161). In him reservation, discretion and deference also reign, an intellect or "sort of councillor, primarily devoted to his egotism, no doubt, but nevertheless functioning as a sort of family solicitor" (AD, 165). In the incipient culture represented by Wilbeck, the chief characteristic of egocentric civilization, self-assertion, is supplanted by "a positive satisfaction in considering others and subordinating that primordial impulse to triumph over them" (AD, 166); "egotistical preposses-sions" are increasingly reduced through "service and contribution to broad human ends" (AD, 187).[21]

Such a psychological adjustment signifies not only the birth of a new culture but the emergence of a new species of mankind from whom that culture originates. In speaking of this new species Wilbeck charactertisti-cally synthesizes Darwinian and Spenglerian ideas.[22] Possibly expanding Spengler's interpretation of culture (I, 18), Wilbeck argues that since the human race does not evolve linearly or accretively, it should be viewed from a Copernican perspective which admits no priority to any one species. "*Homo* . . . is a genus with an immense range of species, sub-species, hybrids and mutations," Wilbeck explains (AD, 174), and like the culture arising from it, each species remains subject to the morphology of birth, growth, decline and death. Differentiating between *Homo Doloresi-form* or *homo regardant* and *Homo Wilbeckius* or *homo rampant*, Wilbeck describes the former as "a widespread, familiar type, emphatic, impulsive," stressing the "traditional, legal and implacable" (AD, 174, 175)—features of the declining phase of Western civilization as defined by Spengler. The latter species, on the other hand, is "probably a recent mutation, observant, inhibited, . . . disingenuous," flexible, imaginative, "open-minded and futuristic" (AD, 174-75)—traits of the cultural phase as defined by Spengler. With increasing conviction Wilbeck comes to believe that he and Dolores "are not really female and male of the same kind, but creatures of a different kind, for whom any mutuality of understanding is forever impossible," even as "the Neanderthaler was different from the Cro-Magnard" (AD, 188, 189). In *The Outline of History* Wells refers to the appearance of the Cro-Magnard as "an enormous leap forward in the history of mankind" (OH, 67), and presumably Wilbeck's analogy suggests that the emergence of *homo rampant* is an equivalent advancement. However, whereas the earlier mutation resulted in disparate physical shapes, the principal difference between the two contemporary species lies in a psychological divergence, in a change "of a mental rather than of a physically visible sort" (AD, 209).

The significance of *homo rampant* as another prodigious transitional factor in the evolution of the human race is expressed in the narrator's instinctive attraction to Rennes, the subject of Wilbeck's opening and closing remarks. Rennes, Wilbeck comments, is "mainly an eighteenth-century town" with an "essential sensual innocence of the seventeenth century," a pre-war place, "very completed" as well as "unhurried and satisfied with itself" (AD, 5, 31, 287). Wilbeck detects a "faint flavour of intimacy with those who had planned and built" Rennes (AD, 284) because the town mirrors the earlier cultural stage of Western civilization; that is, Rennes reflects Western cultural sensuousness and instinct just before they transformed into civilized formality and rationality. Rennes demonstrates that transitional ripening of consciousness which Spengler located for Western culture in the seventeenth and eighteenth centuries and which for *homo rampant* is slowly coming into being through Wilbeck's thoughts. One might say, in the light of Spenglerism, that Rennes and Wilbeck exist contemporaneously in metaphysical time, as if they represented parallel points on two different tiers in the spiral or "womb of time." Interestingly, even as early as *The Outline of History* Wells had interpreted the seventeenth and eighteenth centuries "as an interregnum in the progress of mankind towards a world-wide unity," as a special occasion for the "gathering up of the ideas of men and the resources of science for a wider human effort" (OH, 811, 812).

The narrator's attraction to eighteenth-century Rennes is reinforced by his perception of himself as a Boswellian biographer. He is at once "Boswell observant" and the Johnson-like doer (AD, 38) whom he studies. He explains, "Among other characters that the extroverted Stephen Wilbeck watches with detachment, acute interest and slightly qualified amusement, is . . . a minor character in the Stephen Wilbeck troupe —Stephen Wilbeck, that complicated introvert, the tucked-in part of myself" (AD, 118; cf. 160). Wilbeck bears a synchronic relation to Boswell, as to Rennes, in the spiral of time. Emerging from this "womb of time" characterized by "a magnificent progressive achievement continually opening out" (AD, 176), he represents a somewhat more evolved, yet parallel, mode of their eighteenth-century typicality. And this evolution, as Wilbeck remarks, is "of a mental rather than of a physically visible sort." He is both observer and subject perceived, and his subject's mental rather than physical activity is what he records in his "diary-biography" (AD, 187), a work playfully entitled *Apropos of Dolores* (and so indirectly pointing to the narrator as its subject) and manifesting an evolutionary advancement of the literary type represented by James Boswell's *The Life of Samuel Johnson* (1791).

That Wilbeck's species is a new beginning within a continuum accounts for the water imagery in *Dolores*. This imagery suggests a condition similar to Noah's flood, which as we saw in *All Aboard for Ararat*, Wells interpreted as an emblem for the recurrent transition from a dead to a burgeoning world. Moreover, Darwin's theory of evolution emphasized, as Wells noted in *The Outline of History*, that "there is no sort of land animal in the world . . . whose structure is not primarily that of a water-inhabiting being which has been adapted . . . to life out of the water" (OH, 21). Evolution is continuous in the womb of time and, as Wilbeck remarks, is now "of a mental rather than of a physically visible sort"; time's spiral is a "whirlwind" in Wilbeck's mind (AD, 274) similar to the eddy in Brynhild's mind. So in *Dolores* the transformation implied through allusions to Noah's flood and its related concern of evolutionary emergence from the sea or womb of time is principally associated with the mind. Wilbeck frequently refers to "problems and perplexities *floating* in [his] mind, or lurking unformulated in the *deeps* beneath [his] mind" (AD, 4-5; emphasis added). Wilbeck's mind is inundated by the catastrophic flood of declining Western civilization as represented by Dolores, who readily finds "opportunities for overflow", who talks "in a steady undulating flow," who arouses "a great familiar flood," and who is given to "a torrent of self exposition" (AD, 73, 145, 147, 220). Wilbeck eventually appreciates Foxfield's description of the post-war West as a world deluged by *superfluities*: "there is a superfluity of low-grade activity now in human life, a tremendous gadding about, a superfluity of sexual appetite, a still greater superfluity of the desire for excitement, an accumulation of resentment and restlessness" (AD, 35). Adrift in this flooded world, Wilbeck complains of uncontrolled "fluctuations of mood" in himself and ironically laments late in his narrative, "I steered myself almost as much as a cork in a cataract" (AD, 1, 258).

"We are like early amphibians," Wells observed in his autobiography, "struggling out of the waters that have hitherto covered our kind, into the air, seeking to breath in a new fashion and emancipate ourselves from long accepted and long unquestioned necessities" (EA, 3). A member of a new species emerging amphibianlike (the narrator's image, AD, 279) from the superfluity of the Western world, Wilbeck eventually finds himself "afloat . . . upon a vast theory of his own" (AD, 178) and thinks of his book as a shiplike vehicle preserving his thoughts (evolution is now mental) as they surface from the deluge. Feeling a "current . . . dragging at [his] mental keel," he realizes that his thoughts must either emerge like "bubbles in a fountain" or else "seep away into the general mass" and succumb to an inundation (Wilbeck's word) leaving "man's understanding of life buried deeply under a silt of fear, error and intolerance" (AD, 21, 36, 41, 177). Bubbling new thoughts to the top, as it were, occasions a sense of joy because it signifies the evolutionary birth of Wilbeck's new culture from the womb of time, a birth implying a hope antithetical to decaying civilization's (Dolores') fear of death. From the torrent of the contemporary mental confusion and frustration surging in the human unconscious, Wilbeck's thoughts surface like bubbles or like a cork in a cataract, and slowly they contribute to a shiplike or arklike structure. "I seem to be on something like a ship's bridge," he dreamily observes at one point. Though he is dissatisfied with the metaphor because "it suggests something shaped, rigid and final," he still concludes, "I am helping to build an ark for the human mind" (AD, 177, 280-281). Exemplifying the characteristic humility of *homo rampant* (often he speaks of himself in the third person), Wilbeck adds: "ark-building is a gigantic proposition and I doubt if I am even a foreman riveter on the immense hull such an ark needs to be" (AD, 280).

Appropriately, then, Wilbeck closes his book on a hopeful note as he looks upon a seashore, where the "beach life outside is very pleasant" by "the softly soughing sea" and where "the reflections of people on the wet sand" particularly appeal to him (AD, 273). The scene is virtually without malice, in his opinion, because it depicts the "magnificent progressive achievement continually opening out" of the womb of time and the intimated benignity of this evolutionary process. The people on the wet beach look like amphibians coming ashore, like bubbles at the edge of a fountain—images intimating not only Wilbeck's attraction to Rennes but also his somewhat changed attitude toward Lettice, with whom he was very disappointed (AD, 127, 276) but of whom he thought better when he observed she could swim quite well (AD, 265). Portraying a dramatic transitional point, the beach scene objectifies the evolutionary process evident in the emergence of Wilbeck's thoughts on the shore of his mind.

Modified Spenglerian concepts, in conjunction with modified Freudian and Darwinian notions, influence not only the characterization, motifs, and ideas of *Dolores*, but also the structure of the novel. According to Spengler, art inherently reflects the culture from which it arises, particularly the current stage in the morphology of that culture. Art emanating from the early or cultural phase of a civilization reveals in its style a "rhythm of the process of a self-implementing," whereas "the Civilized style . . . arises as the expression of the state of completeness" and aims for "a splendid perfection" (II, 109). Spengler also distinguishes these two styles in terms of imitation and ornament. By *ornament* he means self-conscious art derived from "an ego conscious of its own specific character"; by *imitation* he means instinctive art "born of the secret rhythm of all things cosmic" (I, 191). In short, civilization institutionalizes the forms of art, while cultural art inherently conveys the universal rhythm of the ceaseless transition of formlessness into form in, as it were, an evolving manner.

The shape of Wilbeck's narrative conforms to the Spenglerian concept of cultural art. Not in intellectual control of his story, Wilbeck writes instinctively in a style rhythmically fluctuating with his moods; the style and diary format of his unsystematic account mirror the "long, loose, unencumbered activities" characteristic of his evolving thoughts (AD, 84). Significantly, Wilbeck's moment of deepest insight comes when he is "a little drunk" and is "writing in [his] sleep" (AD, 176, 178), a time when undirected thoughts bubble up from the depths of his unconscious.

Just as his thoughts emerge from these formless depths and surface into burgeoning consciousness or form, his diarylike narrative inherently exhibits a rhythm typical of cultural art, the rhythm of a creative, evolving design relatively free from the influence of fixed artistic conventions or from conscious authorial control.

This emerging design presses against and revises convention from within, just as *homo rampant* evolves from within the pattern of the species. It is embodied textually in Wells's technique of the splintering frame. This technique is evident not only in the advancement in *Dolores* of the Boswellian biographical type but also in other challenges to reader expectations. The most blatant frustration occurs when the reader completes the novel without discovering for certain whether Wilbeck murdered his wife. Carefully planted clues in the narrative intimate that Wilbeck is quite capable of the deed, clues capped at the very end of the novel by Wilbeck's final ruminations:

> Even if my curious suspicion about that Semondyle is justified; still I have neither regret nor remorse. If I were to be put back to the moment... and went along the corridor to her, would I do it—if I did it—again?
> I would.
> Yes. Even if I did not do it then; now after reflection I should certainly do it quite deliberately. (AD, 289)

This refusal to concede to a reader's expectation of a definitive disposition of the problem as well as the surprising addition of a touch of harshness to an essentially congenial narrator are deliberate. As Wilbeck says of his narrative, and echoing a point Wells made in *Meanwhile*, "it is a picture of a relationship even if it is not a portrait of a person" (AD, 208).

In a sense the reader had been warned very early to abandon normal expectations about the work:

> My notes may have a lot too much theorizing about life and its possibilities in them for your taste, but after all this is my book and not yours. If you confront me with the alternative, I prefer theorizing to pleasing you. You can go to some other book if you do not like this one, or write a book to your own measure. (AD, 41)

This admonition, splintering what might have been a self-containing narrative frame in the novel, implies that the reader who continues to read the novel conspiratorially shares in what is to follow. This reader, identified with the "me and you and all of us" (AD, 160), presumably belongs, like Wilbeck, to *homo rampant* and to some degree participates in the emerging "collective mind" (AD, 213) associated with this species.

The inclusion of reader relativity in this novel is the result of Wells's effort to give *Dolores* a fourth dimension.

This technique of the splintering frame includes the conflict between the sexes that, in Wells's opinion, comprises a convention of the novel. In *Dolores* this conflict is mutated, revised or evolved into a conflict between species: "I do not find any echo of Tolstoy's *Kreutzer Sonata* in our relations," Wilbeck explains about his marital affairs, "I do not think that at the root of it mine is a man-and-woman story at all. It is a story about two different people" (AD, 188). This remark draws attention to the convention involved, stimulating reader awareness of the device; through the implied conspiratorial relationship between narrator and reader, the text finally points to the world in which the reader lives. Since the convention has been mutated, so has the narrative, which Wilbeck explains (recalling his earlier references to Boswell and admonition about theorizing), "was begun not as a story but as an essay" (AD, 209). *Essay* refers not only to the harangue of Foxfield and the disquisitions of Wilbeck violating conventional fictional patterns, not only to Wells's idea of the properly realistic novel as "journalistic" fiction, but also, in its etymological sense, to the processes of examination and trial. *Dolores* is an examination trying to achieve form, is a work begun *"in medias res"* (AD, 245) and revealing a slowly emerging structural "framework" barely "sketched out" (AD, 42). In its struggle to emerge from within fictional conventions and to generate a revised emergent structure, Wilbeck's narrative becomes an essay.

So beneath Wilbeck's cultural art, with its external impression of chaotic detail and apparent formlessness (embodying Wells's technique of the splintering frame), lies a latent inner form, which the inevitable subsequent civilization phase will convert into rigid convention. Because he intuits this underlying emergent principle of order in his apparently discursive and inconsistent (AD, 268) narrative, Wilbeck indeed senses that his thoughts somehow contribute to an emergent arklike structure. He experientially discovers the truth of the Spenglerian notion that every artist "has something in him which, by force of inward necessity, never emerges into consciousness but dominates *a priori* the form-language of his work" (I, 345). This "something" is the internally cohesive and underlying force known as Destiny (I, 353); artistic style is "inaccessible to art-reason, a revelation of the metaphysical order, a mysterious 'must,' a Destiny" (I, 221). By Destiny Spengler means a transcendent Will, "a name, a prime-word like God, a sign for something of which we have an immediate inward certainty but which we are for ever unable to describe" (I, 300). As Wilbeck observes, "there is something real going on, something not ourselves that goes on, in spite of our interpretations and misconceptions. That ultimate reality behind the curtains may be fundamentally and irresolvably multiple and intricate and inexplicable, but it goes on" (AD, 285). For Wells, Spengler's concept of Will coalesces with Schopenhauer's; and this composite notion comprises the heart of Wells's belief in an emergent "collective mind."

The protagonist of *Apropos of Dolores* is named Wilbeck because he beckons to this Will, serves as a mouthpiece of this Will (*bec* [Fr.], meaning beak, nib [pen] or, figuratively, mouth.)[28] At one point observing that human brains "have usurped control of the simple apes we used to be" (AD, 212), Wilbeck gradually realizes that he is essentially a passive agent before this force. If Wilbeck is not, in Schopenhauerian terms, to resist this force and become frustrated (AD, 28-30), of necessity he must voluntarily and actively comply with it. Consequently, Wilbeck not only accepts his role as a "servant of, and a part of, this greater new world that struggles to exist," but also finally actively engages in setting "ideas in order" as human Destiny leads mankind towards "a sort of common mind" (AD, 38, 213, 282). Unable to attain full consciousness of this force, Wilbeck demonstrates a Spenglerian cultural response to his immediate inward certainty of its influence by confessing at the end of his narrative that finally his thoughts reflect "unadulterated mysticism" (AD, 285).

As a mouthpiece of the Will or Destiny, Wilbeck is inwardly compelled to write, to use language. Because the various species of mankind now evolve mentally rather than physically, language is crucial. Language gives form to thoughts emerging amphibianlike from the formless sea of humanity's unconscious. Through words, "the mechanism of a vast abundance of suggestion and enrichment," early man "became more companionable." Today, too, by means of words we fathom "each other's minds in conversation," "see with a new precision and discover beauty" (AD, 283). Destiny, Spengler asserts informs the inner meaning and ordering symbolism beneath the mere syllables of individual words; and likewise Wilbeck concludes: "by getting numbers of people to think as hard as they can and state as clearly as they can, and then by bringing their results together, gradually, a clearing-up is possible"; "to help set ideas in order is therefore the very best work one can do in the world" (AD, 281-82).[24] The word can become flesh.

In his struggle for some self-control and in his effort to give birth or form to formless intuitions submerged in the depths of his unconscious,

Wilbeck realizes that he "must think" and then "write it out" (AD, 269). In this way he begins to be and to know himself (AD, 228), even as the formless intuitions of cultural aesthetics slowly transform into the rational, self-conscious formalities of civilized artistry. Wilbeck's narrative, then, becomes a mirror (like a proper diary) reflecting an inner cohesion and symbolism which only gradually enters into his developing self-consciousness. Together Wilbeck and the reader begin to see beneath the apparent aimlessness of the narrative's sealike prose, with its long, loose and unencumbered quality, "a string of variations on a thread of events" (AD, 286). Wilbeck's book is like a musical composition, in which ideas are explored through contrapuntal arrangement—variations on a theme, ideas mutually, if somewhat elusively, related and intuitively experienced more than rationally comprehended. Music and language comprise two modes of communication capable of stirring people to "stretch out more and more beyond the here and the now." Unwittingly Wilbeck alerts the reader to the significance of the musical structure of his own account when he observes that "we love the mind that speaks to us in music" (AD, 283). For Wells, literature and music were capable of communicating a sense of the fourth dimension (CT, 79).

Wilbeck is the Spenglerian artist in whom the "soul, like the soul of a Culture, is something potential that may actualize itself" (I, 102). His creativity emanates from an interior compulsion submerged within the depths of his unconscious, depths suggestive of the literal sea from which land life evolved, of Noah's deluge symbolizing a new beginning in human life, and of the mystical cosmic ocean or Will comprising the spiral or womb of time. With the demise of Dolores (Western civilization) Wilbeck begins to actualize this potential, gradually ordering his initially formless thoughts into language through a process of emerging consciousness, of the word made flesh, analogous to building an ark. He exemplifies a very early stage in the cultural phase of *homo rampant*, what Spengler refers to as a primitive, childlike "longing, which will presently come into consciousness more and more clearly as a feeling of constant direction" (I, 78). Indeed by the end of his story Wilbeck perceives that his book "has changed considerably in the telling as his tale has unfolded" (AD, 290). Whereas at first he was satisfied to be passively "busy about a mildly varied series of small things" (AD, 31), he now senses in the mirrorlike diary of his narrative hints of a grand Destiny, an inner order or Will operating in and giving a contour to his life.

Apropos of Dolores, then, inherently expresses the cultural phase of a new human species. No artificially contrived structure dominates this book, the internal thematic unity of which emerges amphibianlike from the musical rhythm or variations of the sealike moods of its narrator. The underlying, emerging structure of *Dolores* derives from within the narrative; this structure conveys only an intimated evolutionary shape, a form entirely appropriate to the ideas expressed. It conveys "a transitional form" akin to the transitional evolutionary stage, within the spiral of time, exemplified by its narrator (AD, 283). Wells's reliance upon an unfolding internal structure in this novel conforms to Spengler's remarks about logic: "There is an organic logic, an instinctive, dream-sure logic of all existence as opposed to the logic of the inorganic, the logic of understanding and of things understood" (I, 117). In *Dolores* Wells was still repudiating Jamesian aesthetic principles, but more significantly he was evolving a different species of art. This new species of art, reflecting an adaptation of Spenglerian thought, was in Wells's view appropriate to the new culture of *homo rampant* emerging, in accordance with Destiny or Will, from the depths of the womb of time.

CHAPTER V

Wellsian Logology and Later Fiction

The transcendental optimism, whatever its pessimistic undercurrent, informing Wells's conception of a progressive, potentially beneficent Collective Will is decidedly not modern. On the other hand, his stress on the generative capacity of the human will expressed through language is more contemporary than one might at first expect. Admittedly much of contemporary literature, albeit by no means all of it, inclines toward a Beckettian breakdown of language and a silence in response to the inscrutable absurdity of existence.[1] This is a latter-day development of, say, Herman Melville's sense, especially in *Billy Budd* (completed 1891), of the development of human consciousness, or of philosophical self-reflection, as a fall into the chaos of language. In contrast, whatever tendency toward silence surfaces in Wells's work is engendered by wonder over life's paradoxes—over the inexplicable congruence of "essential complements" in human experience. Consider the example of Huss:

> The thoughts that it seemed to him that God was speaking through his mind, can be put into words only after a certain fashion and with great loss, for they were thoughts about things beyond and above this world, and our words are all made out of the names of things and feelings in this world. Things that were contradictory had become compatible, and things incomprehensible seemed straightforward, because he was in a dream. It was as if the anaesthetic had released his ideas from their anchorage to words and phrases and their gravitation towards sensible realities. (W, 11: 154-155)

Ten years earlier George Ponderevo also struggled with language, and for him the narrative he writes remains as unfocused as "something beautiful, worshipful, enduring" has remained elusive in his life. Both his narrative and his quest for meaning are threatened by a fatal silence, the same silence out of which thought and language are born. Only at the end of his account does he experience the more positive mystical aspect of this silence: "I fell into thought that was nearly formless, into doubts and dreams that have no words, and it seemed good to me to drive ahead and

114

on and on through the windy starlight" (W, 12:273, 530). Thirty-two years later Ponderevo's experience of and Huss's complaint about the limits of language reappear in another of Wells's books:

The speech of *Homo Tewler, Homo sub-sapiens,* is still incapable of expressing reality, and his thought at its clearest is a net of misfitting symbols, analogies and metaphors, by which he hopes to ensnare the truth of his desires. . . . Some day ingenious people may devise ways of bringing language which is not only the expression but the instrument of thought, nearer to verifiable reality. (YC, 169-170)

In contrast to Wells's sense of the inadequacy of language, the tendency toward silence exhibited by contemporary fiction derives from a sense, not of the fullness but of the emptiness of time and space.

Not long ago a group of writers contributed to a revival of the Romantic emphasis on language, particularly the spoken word. Referred to as the Angry Young Men, these authors appreciated the generative capacity of language. Fascination with language emerged, for instance, in the novels of Kingsley Amis, who has explicitly acknowledged his debt to Wells. In Amis' *I Like It Here* (1958), to cite one example, we are told that language is the great social instrument. In novel after novel Amis deftly integrates entertainment and instruction in order to make his fiction instrumental to social improvement. Language figures significantly as well in the title story of Alan Sillitoe's *The Loneliness of the Long Distance Runner* (1959), in which a rebellious narrator, a thief, learns to think in prison; his thoughts lead to self-conscious reflection in the narrator as he discovers/celebrates his cunning in a gaming world. Similarly in Sillitoe's *Saturday Night and Sunday Morning* (1958) Arthur Seaton, a deft liar who believes "the big wide world hasn't heard from" him yet, manifests a rebelliousness of expression and behavior engendered by the thinking he does daily while slaving (like a prisoner) in a factory; specifically he becomes self-aware by means of "violent dialogues flay[ing] themselves to death in his mind as he [goes] on serving a life's penance at the lathe."[2]

John Osborne, who like Amis and Sillitoe has been identified with the Angry Young Men, provides still better examples. In *Look Back in Anger* (1956), which like Osborne's *The Entertainer* (1957) recalls the Edwardian era nostalgically, Jimmy Porter rails against the conditions of modern life; he complains for an entire dissatisfied generation about values all but lost in a dissipated world. If his vehemence lacks direction, he nonetheless shouts himself into being. The new world engendered by the Logos-power of his spoken words exists only within Porter, the angry "saint" who remains impotent in the world at large—a distinct contrast to Wells's belief in the word as transformer of interior insight into exterior possibility, the frame splintered from within. Osborne appears to be more aligned with Wells in *Luther* (1961), in which the Protestant reformer says, "I sat in my heap of pain until the words emerged and opened out," and "I listened for God's voice, but all I could hear was my own." Osborne's Luther recalls Wells's Job Huss, who discovers the will of God in his heart (rather than in his bowels), especially in the words spawned from that heart and its correlative faculty, the imagination. Also reminiscent of Wells's work is Luther's dream of his struggle "to open a gate which would take me out. But the gate was no gate at all. It was simply an open frame."[3] For Osborne, as for Wells, language gives expression to the deepest levels of human experience and presses against as well as expands the current limits, or tiers, of the predestining framework encompassing the human self.

The example of the Angry Young Men suggests that Wells's faith (like George Bernard Shaw's) in the spoken word as possessing a Logos-power is not merely a regression to nineteenth-century Romanticism or, before that, to seventeenth-century Puritanism. In fact Wells's view of language survives in the works of the successors of the Angry Young Men. For instance, in the recent comic novels of Vladimir Nabokov, Ken Kesey, Robert Coover and John Barth, protagonists perceive that language possesses a mythic creative power in the human perception of reality, which is only a fiction; consequently these protagonists use words to create their own reality, an interior new world for themselves.[4] This is an extreme position, of course, and it is not equivalent to Wells's view. Nevertheless, this attitude of certain contemporary authors was anticipated by Wells's belief that just as God is said to have "made the whole world by just saying it" (SB, 7), so too can humanity create new worlds of possibility by verbally expressing humanity's divine-like Collective Will (HT, 123, 213, 262).

This belief in the Logos-power of willful words signifies a major distinction between Wells and Dickens, whom critics have readily and in some respects rightly yoked together for nearly a hundred years. Dickens' characters, in *Our Mutual Friend* (1864) for instance, find themselves trapped within their language, an imprisonment reflecting the confining nature of Victorian society as a whole.[5] Unlike Dickensian characters, with whom they might share other affinities, Wellsian protagonists talk themselves out of social prisons into new mental vistas. A good example of this pattern is the protagonist of *The History of Mr. Polly*, a work generally referred to as heavily influenced by Dickens. With a regenerating

116

primitivisim (W, 17:268) Polly breaks through the meshes of delimiting language as well as of the social and ideological concepts informing that language. In his own "untrained, undisciplined, and spontaneous" manner he speaks himself into being with the simple words "clear out": "When a man has once broken through the paper walls of everyday circumstance, those unsubstantial walls that hold so many of us securely prisoned from the cradle to the grave, he has made a discovery. If the world does not please you, *you can change it*" (W, 17:212). This belief becomes more deftly managed in Wells's fiction as his thought matures, but the thrust remains the same. In *Meanwhile* language is said to constitute "a cathedral of ideas," and Philip Ryland, a protagonist, represents "thousands of people . . . who needed only sufficient stimulation to be released . . . from the sort of verbal anchylosis that had kept him inexpressive" (M, 23, 298). In *The Brothers* Robert Patzel, one of the twin protagonists, learns, "Every man is an assertion or a nonentity" (Bro, 123). And in *Babes in the Darkling Wood* young Stella self-consciously thinks, "I've said something that's been on my mind in a state of helpless solution ever so long. *That*, somehow, has crystallised it" (BD, 12). Given birth by the will and imagination, which participate in the Collective Will, words (as Wells says in *The New Machiavelli*) can awaken one from the sleep of "the thing that is" to the multidimensional dreamlike reality of the "speculative 'if'," which is for Wells (as we have seen) like a succession of circuiting tiers along an ever-expanding spiral of time.

Wells's emphasis upon the Logos-power of language, then, represents a transitional link between, at one end, the Romantic admiration of language and the Victorian approach to language as a reflector of social conditions, and, at the other end, such post-modern writers as the Angry Young Men and various contemporary comic novelists. Wells anticipates the affirmation of values implicit in the use of language by these recent writers, who may also owe a debt to Conrad's *Lord Jim* (1900) and *The Heart of Darkness* (1902), where language is paradoxically deceiving and ennobling even as it functions as an inadequate yet appropriate vehicle for Marlow's ethical concerns. Like the Angry Young Men, Wells looks forward to Jacques Lacan's view of the acquisition of language as a crucial event, an act of creation, constituting a person's achievement of identity. However, Wells remains closer than the Angry Young Men to the Romantic roots of this affirmation and at the same time to the Victorian regard of verbal expression as an ethos of social improvement. A distinct pulsation of despair characterizes the rhythm of the writings of the Angry Young Men, even as Wells's optimism has an undercurrent of

117

pessimism and even, for that matter, as Transcendental Romanticism *per se* cannot fully escape influxes from the darker side of existence. But whereas Wells believes in the possibility of "the word made flesh," the later writers who stress the Logos-power of language tend to confine its generative capacity to the psyche of the individual, who can change nothing in the external world; the fictional world of these later writers remains depleted of meaning and value, merely a manifestation of a metaphysical void swallowing individual voice and identity.

This sense of depletion suggests several more contemporary writers, masters of the anti-novel, called by John Barth the literature of exhaustion. The anti-novel is not new, of course. Sterne's *Tristram Shandy* (1760-67), Wells's favorite work (W, 9:364), is an archetype of the mode, and in the same century Henry Fielding delighted in generic self-referentiality in his novels. Nor was the nineteenth century exempt from a similar sensibility, as witnessed by Thackeray's explicit metaphor of the puppet show, an image encouraging readers, who are distanced from the novel's characters, to think of *Vanity Fair* (1847-48) as an authorially directed fabrication and so to derive their own ethical standard.[6] Wells seized upon this de-constructive element in the tradition of the novel for the purpose of assaulting other conventions of the genre, most specifically the Jamesian illusion of enclosure or self-containment in a work of art. In his intensification of this de-constructive element, particularly by the splintering frame technique evoking an aesthetic fourth dimension, Wells served as a transitional figure to such contemporary practitioners of the literature of exhaustion as Nabokov, who cited Wells as one of the outstanding novelists of this century.

The technique of the splintering frame gave Wells one means of indicating that readers engage with texts as if in a dream and that such dreamy engagement typifies the illusion of their daily lives in the world. The device of the splintering frame, for Wells as for later anti-novelists, ideally awakens the reader from this sleep. Whereas for the later writers, readers are awakened to experience a reality of void, of entropy or (at best) satirical endurance of the impossible, for Wells readers should ideally be roused to perceive a human dimension potentially rich in hope. Wells's manner can be just as abrupt as that of contemporary novelists, but sometimes it is very gentle in effect. When we learn, for example, that the dimension visited by Mr. Barnstaple, in *Men Like Gods*, "was but one of countless universes that move together in time, that lie against one another, endlessly like the leaves of a book" (W, 18:323)—a passage Wells specifically recalled in 1942 (CT, 79)—we suddenly relate differently to the very volume in our hands. The entire *structure* of the book now emblemizes our own existence, as if our life were a mere page in a multi-paged cosmic text or a mere circuit (tier) in a multidimensional spiral of time.

Wells's concept of time and literary structure led, as we have seen, to a typology of characterization. It also resulted in a typology of textual models. Behind this practice lies the notion that just as all human personality types repeat themselves over and over with expanding infinitesimal variation, so too do all modes of writing. In *The Undying Fire* Huss discovers that all books are reduced to one text written, despite different titles and authors over the ages, by one collective person. As a master of the discursive novel, Wells sought literary models which would free him from the need for the philosophically untenable linearity of plot as well as from other conventions of the novel. He preferred models, like *Tristram Shandy*, that could express his relish for novelty and for violating reader expectations. Reviewers were not at all slow to react to this attitude, and they raised questions about just what Wells thought the novel was as a form or whether he was simply dishonest in calling his works novels. But Wells was sure that the novel was protean, the most inclusive of the literary genres (BD, x). Since he was also sure that it ought to be reflective of post-war reality, he effected (a) a fictional surface manifesting a randomness and diffusion confronting expected patterns of orderly development and (b) an inner structure remaining emergent, unfinished and expanding, like the universe. Speaking in 1934 of Dickens, Thackeray and their successors, Wells observed: "In a way they had exhausted the soil for the type of novel they had brought to a culmination," and new classes of readers

> did not understand and enjoy the conventions and phrases of Trollope or Jane Austen, or the genteel satire of Thackeray, they were outside the 'governing class' of Mrs. Humphry Ward's imagination, the somber passions and inhibitions of the Brontë country, or of Wessex or Devonshire had never stirred them, and even the humour of Dickens no longer fitted into their everyday experiences. (EA, 426)

In short, the novel in its Victorian guise seemed to Wells to be exhausted. So for models he turned to other works generally considered outside the novel proper. For instance, *Men Like Gods* revises Bunyan's *Pilgrim's Progress*, *Mr. Blettsworthy on Rampole Island* incorporates the manner of anthropological treatises, *The Autocracy of Mr. Parham* recasts Petronius' *Satyricon*, *The Anatomy of Frustration* modifies a specific literary critical biography of Robert Burton, and *The Holy Terror* relies on Suetonius' *The Twelve Caesars* as one of its points of departure. Sometimes Wells works within the exhausted genre itself, as exemplified by the revision of the ghost-story formula in *The Camford Visitation* (1937) and of his own early science-fiction formula in *Star Begotten*. In this way Wells anticipates the so-called literature of exhaustion movement, which includes, among others, Borges, Nabokov, Calvino, Barth, Pynchon and Barthelme. These writers, it has been argued, pretend that it is nearly impossible to write original fiction and so they write about the exhausted state of literature, thereby paradoxically creating something. Novelists in search of form, they frequently turn to non-fiction (history, biography, literary analysis, political and scientific narrative), to poetry to fairy tales and the like in order to find vehicles to convey their new subject matter and to derive techniques for transcending the current exhausted modes of fiction.[7] This approach to the novel defines Wells's attitude, especially during the Thirties. The major difference between them surfaces in the fact that in managing their texts the literature-of-exhaustion writers point towards the reader in despair of the existence of any meaning outside the closed world of author and text or, at most, of reader and text; whereas Wells points towards the reader in hope of a more fulfilled human existence within an expanding spiral of time.[8]

The literature of exhaustion requires special sensitivity to narrative voice. Wells similarly devoted a sizeable share of his creative energy to this feature of his novels because splintering the frame of a work required modification of narrative frame. He made very effective use of first-person narration, in such works as *The Croquet Player* and *Apropos of Dolores*. Occasionally he experimented with a very modified form of stream-of-consciousness, as in *Mr. Blettsworthy on Rampole Island* and *Brynhild*. He disapproved, however, of the notion that necessarily "the object of the novelist is to keep the reader entirely oblivious of the fact that the author exists—even of the fact that he is reading a book.... the nearer you can come to making him entirely insensitive to his surroundings, the more you will have succeeded."[9] Believing that "no conceivable reason" informed the belief that "there must be no explanation of the ideas animating the characters, and the author himself had to be as invisible and unheard-of as God" (BD, ix), Wells never shared with Ford Madox Ford and Virginia Woolf a complete authorial aloofness from character and reader, the sort of distance which makes it impossible to know what really happened in *The Good Soldier* (1915) or to determine whether James Joyce was sympathetic or ironic in his presentation of Stephen Daedalus in *A Portrait of the Artist as a Young Man* (1916).

Wells prefers the omniscient point of view, though the third person narrative voice of many of his works cannot be directly identified with Wells. Frequently he employs an unidentified "middle" speaker between author and reader; this speaker may be an omnicommunicative narrator (one who knows and reveals all to the reader, who has complete confidence in him) or, as in *Brynhild*, a suppressive omniscient narrator (one who knows but selects what he chooses to tell).[10] Occasionally the latter type, after the manner of Fielding and Sterne, delights in misdirecting the reader in order to provoke thought. This manner is most demonstrable in *You Can't Be Too Careful*, in which Wells vexes even the distinction between the two kinds of omniscient narrator; in this way he demands readers to participate in determining the meaning of the text. Often the voice of a Wells narrative directly addresses the reader by using the word *we* or *our* or *your* in the fashion of some Victorian novelists—Thackeray, for instance—to engage the reader more directly, again to encourage him to think for himself. Sometimes, as in *Christina Alberta's Father*, this voice employs direct address eliciting reader sympathy for the speaker's problems in trying to keep his story under control. This device appears in the work of Sterne and Fielding as well as in such Victorian works as Charlotte Brontë's *Shirley* (1849), the second paragraph of which advises the reader what not to expect. The genuinely innovative feature of the omniscient narration of Wells's fiction emerges when we recall his long-standing interest in the difference between an individual subjective perception of something and a hypothetical absolute view of it. Wells eventually associated the absolute view with the Collective Will, and this connection led him to devalue the stream-of-consciousness technique in favor of the omniscient manner.

This omniscient narrative voice, appealing to a collective readership, gives expression to the Wellsian concept of "Open Conspiracy," the "main arch, the structural frame of my life," Wells explained, and "of supreme importance in [the] picture of my world" (EA, 549). As defined by Wells in the early Thirties, the Open Conspiracy is a largely unconscious, evolutionary "movement of men of ability and understanding towards a world-wide concentrated effort" (WH, 781) to "rescue human society from the net of tradition in which it is entangled and reconstruct it upon planetary lines" (EA, 549). It manifests an organizing Will, in which we participate in "imperceptible degrees" (WH, 297-299, 781); it steadily displaces "mental tangles, egocentric preoccupations, obsessions, misconceived phrases, bad habits of thought, subconscious fears and dreads and plain dishonesty in people's minds" (EA, 702): "The clearer the idea, the better organized the will in the personas of our species, the more hopeful and successful the working of the human ant-hill" (WH, 299). Whether first-person or omniscient, the narrative voices of Wells's late fiction exhibit evolving will and determination. They honestly admit their limitations, asking for support from the reader. Indeed, they are open-ended personalities, intriguing but somewhat undifferentiated—very average and as incomplete as the stories they narrate. A Wellsian narrator often pretends a long-standing familiarity with the reader and presents himself as if he were essentially equivalent to any given reader. On the basis of this implied familiarity he urges the reader to aid him in the completion of his story and of his own personality by participating in the Collective Will and thereby bringing the world outside the frame of the novel toward a greater approximation of perfection. This solicitation and its effect of mingling the world inside and outside the text is managed through the technique of the splintering frame. In short, Wells's narrators are conspiratorial, particularly in their use of *we* in the sense of an implied shared identity between speaker and reader in the Collective Will.

The notion of a Collective Will or of an Open Conspiracy might be far from modern, but the literary experiments Wells conducted on behalf of these concepts certainly are contemporary. Wells's presence in our consciousness of the development of fiction ought not, therefore, to be restricted to an awareness of a nominal influence on, say, C. P. Snow, Kingsley Amis, Jorge Luis Borges, Saul Bellow, or Vladimir Nabokov. He is a presence in his own right, and of all the Edwardians he is the most genuinely transitional figure linking Victorian and later fiction. That transitional role is not vitiated by whatever was wrong-headed in his understanding of Victorian fiction or by whatever in his thought was out of phase with the modern temper. The novels he wrote provide all the testimony required, for they draw from the traditions of eighteenth- and nineteenth-century fiction, and they anticipate the manner of certain modes of post-modern and contemporary fiction. In these later works technique often becomes an end in itself, and Wells certainly never endorses an art-for-art's-sake mentality. Nevertheless, only with tremendous strain can the novel be made to avoid any moral implication, as even Oscar Wilde discovered.[11] The difference finally is one of degree. Wells is less contemporary to the degree that his explicitly therapeutic purpose departs from the aspirations of current novelists, many of whom prefer either to avoid or to imply some (quite possibly ambiguous) remote purpose or ethical message. By uniting a nineteenth-century faith in values with a modern experimentation with fictional form, Wells emerges as a remarkable artist and a truly transitional figure in the development from Victorian to contemporary fiction.

NOTES

PREFACE

1 Bernard Bergonzi, *The Early H. G. Wells* (Manchester: Manchester University Press, 1961) ; David Lodge, *Language of Fiction* (London: Routledge & Kegan Paul, 1966) ; William Bellamy, *The Novels of Wells, Bennett and Galsworthy: 1890-1910* (London: Routledge & Kegan Paul, 1971).

2 Robert Bloom, *Anatomies of Egotism: A Reading of the Last Novels of H. G. Wells* (Lincoln: University of Nebraska Press, 1977) ; Robert Philmus, "Revisions of His Past: H. G. Wells's *Anatomy of Frustration*," *Texas Studies in Literature and Language*, 20 (1978), 249-266.

3 John Huntington usefully focusses on the dialectic between directed and undirected thought, on the co-existence of opposites, in Wells's early fiction: *The Logic of Fantasy: H. G. Wells and Science Fiction* (New York: Columbia University Press, 1982).

4 Robert Philmus and David Y. Hughes, *The Early Writings in Science and Science Fiction by H. G. Wells* (Berkeley: University of California Press, 1975), pp. 204-205; Michael Ryan, "The Act," *Glyph*, 2 (1977), 68.

5 In footnote 102 of *H. G. Wells on the World State* (New Haven: Yale University Press, 1961), p. 107, Warren Wager too simply affirms Wells's antagonism to Hegelian thought. Characteristically Wells denounced schools of thought that in fact he used or adapted in his work. This is the case as well with George Bernard Shaw, whose work Wells knew and whose late assertions against Hegelian dialectic do not square with the demonstrable influence of Hegel's thought on his writings: see Robert F. Whitman, *Shaw and the Play of Ideas* (Ithaca: Cornell University Press, 1977), pp. 119-166.

6 See William J. Scheick, "Fictional Structure and Ethics in the Edwardian, Modern, and Contemporary Novel," *Philological Quarterly*, forthcoming; and Scheick, "Compassion and Fictional Structure: The Example of Bennett and Gissing," *Studies in the Novel*, 15 (1983), 293-313.

7 The degree to which this rapid rise to fame intruded upon Wells's self-consciousness can be gauged by his reaction to a proposal that he and Arnold Bennett collaborate on a play: see my "Marketable Footle: Bennett and Wells's 'The Crime,' " *Cahiers d'Etudes et de Recherches Victoriennes et Edouardiennes*, No. 9/10 (October 1979), pp, 165-180.

[8] See, for example, Geoffrey West, *H. G. Wells: A Sketch for a Portrait* (London: Howe, 1930); Bergonzi, *The Early H. G. Wells*; Jack Williamson, *H. G. Wells: Critic of Progress* (Baltimore: Mirage, 1973); G. P. Wells, ed., *The Last Books of H. G. Wells* (Tiptree, Essex: The H. G. Wells Society, 1968); William J. Scheick, "Reality and the Word: The Last Books of H. G. Wells," *English Literature in Transition*, 12 (1969), 151-154.

[9] See, for instance, Fritjof Capra, *The Tao of Physics: An Exploration of the Parallels Between Modern Physics and Eastern Mysticism* (Berkeley: Shambhala Publications, 1975) and Gary Zukav, *The Dancing Wu Li Masters: An Overview of the New Physics* (New York: Morrow, 1979).

[10] For an analysis of the difficulties and confusions inherent in these terms see Gerhard Hoffman, Alfred Hornung and Rüdiger Kunow, " 'Modern,' 'Postmodern' and 'Contemporary' as Criteria for the Analysis of 20th Century Literature," *Amerikastudien*, 22, i (1977), 19-46.

CHAPTER I

[1] Bernard Bergonzi, *The Early H. G. Wells* (Manchester: Manchester University Press, 1961), p. 22. Warren Wagar explicitly notes his agreement with Bergonzi on this point, in "Art and Thought," *Virginia Quarterly Review*, 45 (1969), 695. See also Bergonzi, *The Turn of a Century: Essays on Victorian and Modern English Literature* (London: Macmillan, 1973), p. 75.

[2] Mark Schorer, "Technique as Discovery" (1948), in *A Grammar of Literary Criticism*, ed. Lawrence Sargent Hall (New York: Macmillan, 1965), pp. 374-387.

[3] Lucille Herbert, "*Tono-Bungay*: Tradition and Experiment," *Modern Language Quarterly*, 33 (1972), 140-155.

[4] Kenneth B. Newell, *Structure in Four Novels by H. G. Wells* (The Hague: Mouton, 1968); and my "The Thing That Is and the Speculative If: The Pattern of Several Motifs in Three Novels by H. G. Wells," *English Literature in Transition*, 11 (1968), 67-78.

[5] See my "Reality and the Word: The Last Books of H. G. Wells," *English Literature in Transition*, 12 (1969), 151-154; "If Not a Window, at Least a Peephole," *English Literature in Transition*, 13 (1970), 86-88.

[6] Herbert, p. 142.

[7] Virginia Woolf, "Mr. Bennett and Mrs. Brown," *Collected Essays* (New York: Harcourt, Brace & World, 1967), I, 331.

[8] Seymour Chatman, *Story and Discourse: Narrative Structure in Fiction and Film* (Ithaca: Cornell University Press, 1978), p. 49. See also Wolfgang Iser, *The Act of Reading: A Theory of Aesthetic Response* (Baltimore: John Hopkins University Press, 1978).

[9] See Max Webb, "The Missing Father and the Theme of Alienation in H. G. Wells's *Tono-Bungay*," *English Literature in Transition*, 18 (1975), 246.

[10] John R. Reed, *Victorian Conventions* (Athens: Ohio University Press, 1975), p. 39.

[11] Reed, p. 511, note 10.

[12] Bergonzi, p. 121.

[13] William Bellamy, *The Novels of Wells, Bennett and Galsworthy: 1890-1910* (London: Routledge and Kegan Paul, 1971), p. 127.

[14] Darko Suvin, *Metamorphoses of Science Fiction: On the Poetics and History of a Literary Genre* (New Haven: Yale University Press, 1979), p. 208.

[15] Lawrence Jay Dessner, "H. G. Wells, Mr. Polly, and the Uses of Art," *English Literature in Transition*, 16 (1973), 121-134.

[16] On Kipps see Patrick Parrinder, *H. G. Wells* (Edinburgh: Oliver & Boyd, 1970), pp. 87-102.

[17] See, especially, *Henry James and H. G. Wells*, eds. Leon Edel and Gordon N. Ray (Urbana: University of Illinois Press, 1958) and, most recently, Linda R. Anderson, "Self and Society in H. G. Wells's *Tono-Bungay*," *Modern Fiction Studies*, 26 (1980), 199-212.

[18] Joseph Wood Krutch, *The Modern Temper* (1929) (New York: Harcourt, Brace & World, 1956), pp. 168-169.

[19] Archibald Henderson, *George Bernard Shaw: Man of the Century* (New York: Appleton Century Crofts, 1956), p. 791.

[20] In the novels he wrote during the Twenties and Thirties Wells shared with many of his articulate contemporaries the view that the pre-War framework of values had been demolished and, like many of these spokesmen, he was by 1920 skeptical—there had always been an undercurrent of doubt in his work—that science could redeem mankind. He was out of phase with "the modern temper," however, in that he still valued scientific method, the "scientific" rational mind, and the nearly mystical capacity of the human heart to transform humanity.

[21] Edwin A. Abbott, *Flatland: A Romance of Many Dimensions* (1884) (New York: Dover, 1952), p. 88.

[22] H. G. Wells, "Fiction," *Saturday Review*, 80 (1896), 513-514.

[23] Georges Poulet, *Studies in Human Time*, trans. Elliott Coleman (Baltimore: Johns Hopkins University Press, 1956); Margaret Church, *Time and Reality: Studies in Contemporary Fiction* (Chapel Hill: University of North Carolina Press, 1963); Shiv K. Kumar, *Bergson and the Stream of Consciousness Novel* (New York: New York University Press, 1963); W. J. Harvey, *Character in the Novel* (Ithaca: Cornell University Press, 1965); Jerome Hamilton Buckley, *The Triumph of Time: A Study of*

the Victorian Concepts of Time, History, Progress, and Decadence (Cambridge: Harvard University Press, 1966) ; Morris Beja, *Epiphany in the Modern Novel* (Seattle: University of Washington Press, 1971) ; A. A. Mendilow, *Time and the Novel* (New York: Humanities Press, 1972) ; and David Leon Higdon, *Time and English Fiction* (London: Macmillan, 1977). Wells frequently refers to the work of William James.

24 Gertrude Stein, *Picasso* (London: Batsford, 1938), p. 12; Linda Dalrymple Henderson, "A New Facet of Cubism: 'The Fourth Dimension' and 'Non-Euclidean Geometry' Reinterpreted," *The Art Quarterly*, 34 (1971), 411-433; Henderson, "The Merging of Time and Space: 'The Fourth Dimension' in Russia from Ouspensky to Malevich," *The Structuralist*, No. 15/16 (1975-76), pp. 97-108.

25 Guillaume Apollinaire, *The Cubist Painters*, trans. Lionel Abel (New York: Wittenborn, Schulz: 1949), p. 45; Maurice Raynal, "Qu'est ce que ... le 'Cubisme'?" *Cubism*, ed. Edward F. Fry (New York: McGraw Hill, 1966), pp. 129-130 (italics added).

26 Robert Philmus and David Y. Hughes, *The Early Writings in Science and Science Fiction by H. G. Wells* (Berkeley: University of California Press, 1975), p. 60.

27 Robert M. Philmus, "The Time Machine; or, the Fourth Dimension as Prophecy," *PMLA*, 84 (1969), 530-535.

28 Bernard Bergonzi, *The Situation of the Novel* (London: Macmillan, 1970), p. 197. But, one should note, Wells is more interested than his contemporaries generally in temporalizing narrative rather than in the spatialization of form per se. That is to say, Wells is less concerned with what Joseph Frank has discerned as the modern author's fascination with fixing the reader's attention to a limited time area while the time flow of the narrative is halted: see Frank's *The Widening Gyre: Crisis and Mastery in Modern Literature* (New Brunswick: Rutgers University Press, 1963).

29 In *The Turn of the Novel* (New York: Oxford University Press, 1966) Alan Friedman defines "open form" as a manner which is designed to leave the flux of conscience uncontained and to avoid limiting experience. An even more satisfying definition of "open structure" appears in Sharon Spencer's *Space, Time and Structure in the Modern Novel* (New York: New York University Press, 1971), pp. 51-74. See also James Gindon, *Harvest of a Quiet Eye: The Novel of Compassion* (Bloomington: Indiana University Press, 1971).

30 Edel and Ray (eds.), *Henry James and H. G. Wells*, p. 264.

31 Philmus and Hughes, *The Early Writings*, p. 94.

32 Philmus and Hughes, *The Early Writings*, p. 139. See also Roslyn D. Haynes's discussion of Wells's attitudes toward individuality and collectiveness, personal freedom and species predestination, and typical members representing the entire species, in *H. G. Wells: Discoverer of the*

Future (New York: New York University Press, 1980), pp. 118, 125, 132, 167. The best discussion to date of Wells's conception of human will appears in John R. Reed's *The Natural History of H. G. Wells* (Athens: Ohio University Press, 1982), pp. 135-176.

[33] H. G. Wells, "Jude the Obscure," *Saturday Review* 81 (1896), 153-154. More recent commentary on Hardy's typology of characters appears in Virginia R. Hyman's *Ethical Perspective in the Novels of Thomas Hardy* (Port Washington, N.Y.: Kennikat, 1975) and Geoffrey Thurley's *The Psychology of Hardy's Novels* (Atlantic Highlands, N.J.: Humanities Press, 1975).

[34] H. G. Wells, "The Novel of Types," *Saturday Review*, 81 (1896), 23-24.

[35] See my *The Slender Human Word: Emerson's Artistry in Prose* (Knoxville: University of Tennessee Press, 1978), pp. 137-144.

[36] Terry Eagleton, *Marxism and Literary Criticism* (Berkeley: University of California Press, 1976), p. 29.

[37] See Erich Auerbach, *Scenes from the Drama of European Literature* (New York: Meridian, 1959), pp. 53-60; and my "Typology and Allegory: A Comparative Study of George Herbert and Edward Taylor," *Essays in Literature*, 2 (1975), 76-86.

[38] See *Literary Uses of Typology from the Late Middle Ages to the Present*, ed. Earl Minor (Princeton: Princeton University Press, 1977).

[39] Herbert L. Sussman, *Fact into Figure: Typology in Carlyle, Ruskin, and the Pre-Raphaelite Brotherhood* (Columbus: Ohio State University Press, 1979); Jerome Bump, *Gerard Manly Hopkins* (Boston: Twayne, 1982).

[40] Arthur S. Eddington, *Stellar Movements and the Structure of the Universe* (London: Macmillan, 1914), p. 244. Eddington's theory of relativity, incidentally, differs from Einstein's, but Wells does not indicate any awareness of the distinctions.

[41] See M. H. Abrams, *Natural Supernaturalism* (New York: Norton, 1971); and Timothy Materer, *Vortex: Pound, Eliot, and Lewis* (Ithaca: Cornell University Press, 1979).

[42] Georges Poulet, "Timelessness and Romanticism," *Journal of the History of Ideas* 15 (1954), 3-22.

[43] J. Hillis Miller, *The Form of Victorian Fiction: Thackeray, Dickens, Trollope, George Eliot, Meredith, and Hardy* (Notre Dame: University of Notre Dame Press, 1968), p. 33.

[44] Documentation of this point is provided in my "The Thing That Is and the Speculative If," pp. 67-78.

[45] Philmus and Hughes, *The Early Writings*, p. 6.

[46] See Donald David Stone, *Novelists in a Changing World: Meredith, James, and the Transformation of English Fiction in the 1880's* (Cambridge: Harvard University Press, 1972). See also Rubin Rabinovitz, *The*

Reaction Against Experiment in the English Novel, 1950-1960 (New York: Columbia University Press, 1967).

⁴⁷ Walter Pater, *Appreciations*, in *Works* (London: Macmillan, 1915), 5: 66.

CHAPTER II

¹ This chapter is a revision of an essay which first appeared as "The Fourth Dimension in Wells's Novels of the 1920's," *Criticism*, 20 (1978), 167-190.

² Frederic Jameson, *Marxism and Form* (Princeton: Princeton University Press, 1971), p. 341.

³ Ellen Frank, *Literary Architecture: Essays Toward a Tradition* (Berkeley: University of California Press, 1979), p. 212.

⁴ Dagobert Frey, *Gotik und Renaissance als Grundlagen der Modenen Weltanschauung* (Augsburg: Baden bei Wien, 1929), p. 75. In his autobiography Wells refers to *Joan and Peter* (1918) "as shamelessly unfinished as a Gothic cathedral" (EA, 420); cf. "The Contemporary Novel" (W, 9:367). Concerning the influence of Gothic architecture on Victorian fiction, see Peter Conrad, *The Victorian Treasure House* (London: Collins, 1973), pp. 133-175.

CHAPTER III

¹ The following remarks on *The Autocracy of Mr. Parham* are based on an earlier version appearing in "Lost Places in Dreams and Texts: Wells's *The Autocracy of Mr. Parham*," *The Kentucky Review*, 4 (1983), 56-64.

² Several other implications of this paradox are noted in Roslynn D. Haynes's *H. G. Wells: Discoverer of the Future* (New York: New York University Press, 1980), pp. 163-196.

³ See Edward Engelberg, "Escape from the Circles of Experience: D. H. Lawrence's *The Rainbow* as a Modern *Bildungsroman*," *PMLA*, 78 1963), 103-113.

⁴ See Jerome Hamilton Buckley, "H. G. Wells: The Hero as Scientist," in *Season of Youth: The Bildungsroman from Dickens to Golding* (Cambridge: Harvard University Press, 1974), pp. 186-203; and Max Webb, "The Missing Father and the Theme of Alienation in H. G. Wells's *Tono-Bungay*," *English Literature in Transition*, 18 (1975), 246.

⁵ Wells's reaction to Hope's romance is recorded in "Popular Writers and Press Critics: An Informal Appreciation," *Saturday Review*, 81 (1896), 145-146.

⁶ Robert M. Philmus, "Revisions of His Past: H. G. Wells's *Anatomy of Frustration*," *Texas Studies in Literature and Language*, 20 (1978), 253, 259.

7 H. G. Wells, "Fiction," *Saturday Review*, 79 (1895), 556-557.

8 See *Saturday Review*, 79 (1895), 703-704; 80 (1895), 513-514, 735-736. For an excellent study of Poe and Wells, see Catherine Rainwater, "Encounters with the 'White Sphinx': Poe's Influence on Some Early Works of H. G. Wells," *English Literature in Transition*, 26 (1983), 35-51.

9 From a manuscript in the Wells collection held by the Humanities Research Center of the University of Texas at Austin, which has given permission to have the item printed here.

10 Wells expresses these values in two reviews which do not specifically mention Poe: *Saturday Review*, 82 (1896), 32-33; 81 (1895), 48-49.

11 Robert M. Philmus makes this observation in "H. G. Wells as Literary Critic for the *Saturday Review*," *Science-Fiction Studies*, 4 (1977), 172.

12 This formula is described in Jack Sullivan's *Elegant Nightmares: The English Ghost Story from Le Fanu to Blackwood* (Athens: Ohio University Press, 1978), pp. 130-132. An earlier version of my remarks here appeared as "Exorcising the Ghost Story: Wells's *The Croquet Player* and *The Camford Visitation*," *Cahiers d'Etudes et de Recherches Victoriennes et Edouardiennes*, No. 17 (1983), 52-62.

13 John R. Reed makes a distinction between ghost and occult novels in *Victorian Conventions* (Athens: Ohio University Press, 1975), p. 450.

14 See my "The Problem of Origination in Brown's *Ormond*," *Critical Essays on Charles Brockden Brown*, ed. Bernard Rosenthal (Boston: G. K. Hall, 1981), pp. 126-141.

15 H. G. Wells, "Fiction," *Saturday Review*, 79 (1895), 556-557.

16 An earlier version of my comments on this novel appeared in "Towards the Ultra-Science-Fiction Novel: Wells's *Star Begotten*," *Science-Fiction Studies*, 8 (1981), 19-25.

17 For Hegel the truly perfected work of art remains elusive because the achievement of a form perfectly adequate to its content would constitute art's transcendence of itself into Absolute Spirit. See Frederic Jameson, *Marxism and Form* (Princeton: Princeton University Press, 1971), p. 331.

18 It should be remembered that during this time Wells stressed the education of youth above all else in the regeneration of mankind. See John R. Reed, *The Natural History of H. G. Wells* (Athens: Ohio University Press, 1982), pp. 111-133.

19 I have emphasized only these two features. In fact Wells's reach ranges farther and includes, for example, a revision of Olaf Stapledon's *Last and First Men* (p. 81) and, as in *The Anatomy of Frustration* and elsewhere, of Friedrich Nietzche's concept of the *Übermensch* (p. 87). (Stapledon replied in "Mr. Wells Calls in the Martians," *London Mercury* 36 [July 1937], 295-296.) Wells's possible debt to George Du Maurier's *The Martian* (1897) is suggested by John R. Reed, *Natural History*, p. 216.

CHAPTER IV

[1] Norman and Jeanne Mackenzie, *H. G. Wells: A Biography* (New York: Simon and Schuster, 1973), pp. 406-409. See also Lovat Dickson, *H. G. Wells: His Turbulent Life and Times* (New York: Atheneum, 1969), p. 13 and Norman Nicholson, *H. G. Wells* (London: Barker, 1950), p. 88.

[2] Harold Strauss, "Wells Renounces (?) Prophecy and Writes a Good Novel," *New York Times Book Review*, 12 September 1937, p. 3; Richard Vaughan, "Mr. Wells Wiggles His Ears," *New Republic*, 92 (29 September 1937), 222.

[3] For example, David Garnett, "Books in General," *New Statesman and Nation*, 16 (8 October 1938), 532 and Alfred Kazin, "Mr. Wells's Novel," *New York Times Book Review*, 30 October 1938, p. 7.

[4] An earlier version of my remarks on *Brynhild* appeared in "Schopenhauer, Maori Symbolism, and Wells's Brynhild," *Studies in the Literary Imagination*, 13 (1980), 17-29.

[5] *Anatomies of Egotism: A Reading of the Last Novels of H. G. Wells* (Lincoln: University of Nebraska Press, 1977), p. 98.

[6] *The World as Will and Idea*, trans. R. B. Haldane and J. Kemp (London: Kegan Paul, Trench, Trubner, 1891), II, 406. Subsequent volume and page references to this edition will be included parenthetically in the text.

[7] Ettie A. Rout, *Maori Symbolism* (London: Kegan Paul, Trench, Trubner, 1926), p. xxx. Rout acknowledges indebtedness to Wells's *The Outline of History*, and Wells pays tribute to her in *You Can't Be Too Careful* (p. 112).

[8] Rout, p. 199; cf. pp. 205, 213.

[9] Cf. Rout, p. 141.

[10] See, for example, *Times Literary Supplement*, 8 September 1937, p. 673.

[11] Rout, p. 206.

[12] See, for example, Bry, 185, 189, 258, 263, 265, 268. The problem posed by the past informs Wells's satiric treatment of the connection between the Druids and contemporary clerics (Bry 5), of the May Day ceremonial dress (Bry 19), and of the game of charades (Bry 119, 133).

[13] This image is parodied, with irony, in Rowland's Swedenborgian "dream of tiers above tiers of exalted beings," of "circle above circle. He also had his place in one of these tiers serving the ineffable, the transcending, the ultimate beauty" (Bry 49-50).

[14] See Carl Gustav Jung's discussion of mandala symbolism in *The Archetypes and the Collective Unconscious*, trans. R. F. C. Hull (Princeton: Princeton University Press, 1968).

[15] Bernard Bergonzi, *The Early H. G. Wells: A Study of the Scientific Romances* (Manchester: Manchester University Press, 1961), pp. 4-8.

131

[16] *The Decline of the West,* trans. Charles Francis Atkinson (New York: Knopf, 1957), I, 309. Subsequent page references to this work are cited parenthetically in the text; and italics have been deleted. In *Apropos of Dolores* Wells may have his narrator echo Spengler's view (p. 6).

[17] W. Warren Wager mentions this observation in passing in *H. G. Wells and the World State* (New Haven: Yale University Press, 1961), p. 142. An earlier, somewhat different version of my discussion of *Dolores* appeared in "The Womb of Time," *English Literature in Transition,* 18 (1975), 217-228.

[18] Wells has in mind *The War That Will End War* (1914) and *The Salvaging of Civilization* (1921).

[19] At one level Dolores personifies France (AD, 171, 187, 236, 237), which Wells thought had, after World War I, stressed its own national security and advancement at the price of world peace (FM, 58). In lieu of a future-oriented policy of reconciliation with Germany, France, in Wells's opinion, egocentrically asserted a past-oriented policy of ambition, animosity and retaliation. Remember too that during the war the cause of France was identified with the cause of civilization.

[20] Will Durant, *The Story of Philosophy* (Garden Ctiy, N.Y.: Garden City Pub. Co., 1933), p. 324.

[21] I limit to this note several remarks about the third component of the self, what Freud calls the *ego,* what Spengler refers to as *longing,* and what Wilbeck speaks of as the *heart.* Just as the id and the superego require the ego of Freud's system, the ego and the intellect require the heart in Wilbeck's trinity; and it is the longing of the heart, symbolized by Lettice, which comprises the "invisible third angle ... in the marital psychology of the Wilbeck couple" (AD, 119). Unlike Dolores' emphasis on the past and Wilbeck's stress on the future, Lettice focuses on the present (AD, 239). She evinces "a passionate going out to a particular loveliness for its own sake," most notably in her devotion to her lover—an experience Wilbeck also has when he irrationally pursues a strange woman who symbolizes for him that "this universe has something profounder and intenser than its everyday events" (AD, 269, 270). Concerning the three components of the self, Wilbeck concludes that in the "three-fold quandry between brain, egotism and heart" the first urges creative organization, the second requires destructive power and the third desires loveliness and restful entertainment: "Plainly the best recipe for a working compromise with life must be to obey our reason as far as we can ... sublimate our deep seated instinct for malicious mischief, and gratify what we can of our heart's desire, so far as and in such manner as, our consciences approve" (AD, 279, 280). Egotism may be the "foundation stuff of humanity," but "truth [intellect] and loveliness [heart] are primary things" as well (AD, 285).

[22] Spengler, however, did not think of his notions as compatible with those of Darwin, and during the Twenties others used his views to refute argu-

ments based on a belief in Darwinian progress. Darwin, in Spengler's opinion, stressed causality and so expressed a "civilized" reading of biology (I, 120, 121, 369). Wells, of course, thought highly of Darwinian ideas, as he did those of Freud: "These two men are cardinal not so much on account of the actual elucidation they produced but because of the questions they asked and the method of their questioning" (FM, 10). Here again we see Wells's interest in dialectical procedure, and we ought also to recall that in effect Wells was often more Lamarckian than Darwinian in his conception of cultural evolution.

²³ The name Stephen is also significant. Referring to the first Christian martyr, it participates in a religion motif (including references to St. Paul, the Fall, the Old and the New Adam, Calvary, Catholicism, among others) appearing throughout the novel and reinforcing Spenglerian themes. On one occasion Wilbeck, who presents himself as a latter-day "evolved" St. Paul, remarks: "I have had as much of a vision as any of the saints" (AD, 270).

²⁴ In *The Outline of History* Wells remarks how advancements in world communication urge larger political organization (p. 1087). Spenger also argued for the relationship between language and higher world consciousness (I, 55).

CHAPTER V

¹ Ihab Habib Hassan, *Literature of Silence* (New York: Knopf, 1967); Hassan, *The Dismemberment of Orpheus: Toward a Postmodern Literature* (London: Oxford University Press, 1971).

² Alan Sillitoe, *Saturday Night and Sunday Morning* (New York: Signet, 1960), pp. 190, 176.

³ John Osborne, *Luther* (New York: Signet, 1963), pp. 76, 123, 19. In *George Orwell: Fugitive from the Camp of Victory* (Carbondale: Southern Illinois University Press, 1962), Richard Rees in passing places the Angry Young Men between Wells and Orwell.

⁴ See Ronald Wallace, *The Last Laugh: Form and Affirmation in the Contemporary American Novel* (Columbia: University of Missouri Press, 1979).

⁵ Miller, *Form of Victorian Fiction*, p. 93.

⁶ See Wolfgang Iser, *The Implied Reader* (Baltimore: Johns Hopkins University Press, 1974).

⁷ See John O. Stark, *The Literature of Exhaustion: Borges, Nabokov, and Barth* (Durham: Duke University Press, 1974).

⁸ Wells also anticipated the New Journalism: see Richard Hauer Costa, "Edwardian Intimations of the Shape of Fiction to Come: Mr. Britling/Job Huss as Wellsian Central Intelligences," *English Literature in Transition*, 18 (1975), 229-242. Cf. John Hollowell, *Fact and Fiction: The New*

Journalism and the Nonfiction Novel (Chapel Hill: University of North Carolina Press, 1977).

[9] Ford Madox Ford, *Joseph Conrad: A Personal Remembrance* (London: Duckworth, 1924), p. 186.

[10] A good discussion of these two different types of omniscient narration appears in Meir Sternberg's *Expositional Modes and Temporal Ordering in Fiction* (Baltimore: Johns Hopkins University Press, 1978), pp. 236-275. On the role of narrator as character in nineteenth-century fiction, see U. C. Knoepflmacher, *Laughter and Despair: Readings in Ten Novels of the Victorian Era* (Berkeley: University of California Press, 1971).

[11] See John Allen Quintus, "The Moral Implications of Oscar Wilde's Aestheticism," *Texas Studies in Literature and Language,* 22 (1980), 559-574.

www.ingramcontent.com/pod-product-compliance
Lightning Source LLC
Chambersburg PA
CBHW061829040426
42447CB00012B/2889